An APL Compiler

Timothy Budd

An APL Compiler

With 15 Illustrations

Springer-Verlag
New York Berlin Heidelberg
London Paris Tokyo

Timothy Budd
Department of Computer Science
Oregon State University
Corvallis, Oregon 97331
USA

Library of Congress Cataloging-in-Publication Data
Budd, Timothy.
An APL compiler.
Bibliography: p.
Includes index.
1. APL (Computer program language) 2. Compilers
(Computer programs) I. Title.
QA76.73.A27B83 1988 005.13'3 87-28507

Camera-ready copy provided by the author.

9 8 7 6 5 4 3 2 1

ISBN-13:978-0-387-96643-4 e-ISBN-13:978-1-4612-3806-5
DOI: 10.1007/978-1-4612-3806-5

Preface

It was Richard Lipton, my graduate advisor, who in 1977 first discussed with me the simple idea that eventually grew into the APL compiler. At the time, he was on leave from Yale University, where I was working towards my doctorate, and spending a year at the University of California at Berkeley. While we were at Berkeley a student named Brownell Charlstrom and I developed a system using threaded code on a PDP-11 that experimented with some of Dick's ideas. Unfortunately, the system was difficult to use, and the threaded code was not as fast as we had hoped. Interest waned, and the project languished.

In 1980, having finished my dissertation work at Yale, I accepted a position at the University of Arizona and once more started to think about the problem of generating code for an APL-like language. In time I developed another system, the first of many versions of the APL compiler. Although the broad outline of the technique that Dick had proposed remained the same, and indeed remained throughout the project, in detail almost everything changed. Instead of producing threaded code, I generated actual executable code. Since I didn't want to bother with low-level machine details, I selected C as my target language. Instead of using a vector of subscript positions to represent an element I wanted to generate, I used an index into the raveled representation of an expression. By these and many other changes I was finally able to generate code that was considerably faster in execution than the threaded code system developed at Berkeley. However, with the change in request format from a vector of subscript positions to an index into the ravel ordering of the result a few functions, notably the transpose functions, caused problems, and I was eventually forced to use a system in which some requests were presented using vectors and some using indices (this demand driven, space efficient, code generation technique is described in more detail in Chapters 3 through 7).

At about this time I became aware of a paper that was presented by Leo Guibas and Douglas Wyatt at the Fifth ACM Principles of Programming Languages Conference in Tucson, Arizona. They had a novel method for generating code for just the APL functions, the transpose functions, that were causing me trouble. I also acquired a student, Joseph Treat, who was working towards his masters degree at the University of Arizona. I set Joe to reading the Guibas/Wyatt paper, and shortly afterwards he was able to integrate their method into the APL compiler. Thus, we were finally able to eliminate totally the vector form of element request, and the compiler started to take on its present form. Joe continued looking at various implementation issues for another year, among other things implementing the dataflow analysis system described in Chapter 2. Then Joe graduated, the grant funding ran out, and once more the project languished.

In 1985 I took a leave of absence from the University of Arizona and spent time at the Centrum voor Wiskunde en Informatica in Amsterdam, The Netherlands. While there I was contacted by Dr. Sandor Suhai, from the Deutsches Krebsforschungszentrum in Heidelberg. He was interested in my work on APL and invited me to Heidelberg to give a talk. While I am almost certain that the software I gave to Dr. Suhai did not suit his needs (he was looking for a more commercial product, not the type of software, and nonexistent support, that you get in a typical software research project), his invitation did have the effect of forcing me to review the APL compiler project in its entirety. In so doing I concluded that the time was right (indeed, overdue) to describe the whole project in one place, instead of the myriad small papers that we had published from time to time outlining various aspects of the project. This book is the result.

I have already mentioned most of the people to whom I owe acknowledgements. To Dick, Joe, and Dr. Suhai I am of course most grateful. I wish to thank Alan Perlis for showing me, during my graduate school years, just exactly how intellectually challenging and powerful this strange language APL could be. I also wish to thank Lambert Meertens, my nominal supervisor for my year in Amsterdam, for permitting me to work on this manuscript despite whatever personal feelings he might have had towards the language APL. I thank Marion Hakanson for getting the troff typesetting system working for me at OSU. Finally, a few people have made a number of useful comments on earlier drafts of this manuscript: In particular, I wish to thank Ed Cherlin and Rick Wodtli.

Some readers might be interested in obtaining the code for the APL compiler. I distribute the source, subject to the usual caveats found in academically developed software; namely, that it is distributed on an as-is basis, with no guarantee of support, nor any guarantee of its suitability for any use whatsoever. As our interests were in research in code generation and not in developing a commercial quality APL system, there are some features, even some rather basic features, that one might expect to find in an APL system that are missing from our system. These are described in more detail in Appendix 1. Because of these omissions, and because we cannot afford to offer any support for a system that is undoubtedly, despite our best efforts, still buggy, the APL compiler as it stands now is potentially of only limited utility for other purposes. If, despite these warnings, individuals are still interested in obtaining the system, they can write to me at the following address for details.

Tim Budd
Department of Computer Science
Oregon State University
Corvallis, Oregon
97331

Contents

Chapter 1

Why A Compiler ?

The language APL presents a number of novel problems for a compiler writer: weak variable typing, run time changes in variable shape, and a host of primitive operations, among others. For this reason, many people have over time voiced the opinion that a compiler for the language was inherently impossible and that only an interpreter provided the necessary flexibility. One result of the APL compiler project described here is to cast a great deal of doubt on this position.

Our intention in developing a compiler for the language APL had less to do with an affinity for the language APL *per se* than with a desire to investigate the issues raised by the development of a compiler for a very high level language. The aim of the APL compiler project was to investigate whether nontrivial compiled code could be produced for an APL-like language, which we called APLc. The adjective APL-*like* is important here. Since our interest was in code generation and not in producing yet another APL system, we felt at liberty to change certain of the basic features of the language if doing so would result in the compiler being able to generate significantly better code and would not destroy the essential *APLness* of the language. The latter is, of course, a very subjective opinion, and it is certainly true that there are some in the APL community who feel that any change in the basic semantics of the language produces something that is not APL. Nonetheless, it is the opinion of the author that the language APLc is still recognizably (or, some might say, unrecognizably) APL.

The essential features of APL that we sought to preserve in developing the APL compiler were:

1. The use of arbitrary size, homogeneous arrays as a basic datatype, and
2. The set of functions that one associates with APL for operating on such arrays.

Among the features of the language APL that we felt free to meddle with in developing APLc were the following:

1. The elimination of dynamic scoping in favor of static scoping. It was our experience that few APL programmers use dynamic scoping, and it did complicate many of the algorithms that we were interested in. Since it seemed only a marginal issue in the larger problem of code generation, we removed it. [Lisp is another major computer language that utilizes dynamic scoping. It is interesting to note that recent dialects of Lisp, such as Scheme (Abelson 1985) and T (Slade 1987), have also replaced this feature with static scoping].
2. A change in the order of evaluation rules. Although we retain the syntactic rule that says that the right argument of a function is the whole expression to its right, this does not imply necessarily that the right argument will be evaluated before the left. Some functions, for example reshape, will evaluate their left argument prior to examining the right. Although this differs from many APL implementations, it is actually what the APL standard calls a "consistent extension" of the language.
3. The introduction of lazy evaluation semantics. Consider an expression such as:

   $$0\ 1\ /\ 6\ 6 \div 0\ 3$$

   The usual APL semantics would insist upon an error being reported when 6 was divided by 0. The lazy evaluation technique that we wanted to use in the APL compiler would not report this error, since the result would never be used, having been compressed out. Again, the APL standard permits this interpretation as a consistent extension.

4. The introduction of (largely optional) declarations. It was necessary to introduce some declarations in order to determine the meaning of ambiguous tokens at compile time and thus insure a proper parse of a program. Conventional interpreter systems avoid this problem by not assigning meanings to certain tokens until just prior to execution, something a compiler cannot do. Having opened the doors this much, we went on to allow further optional declarations to give hints to the compiler concerning variable type and rank, thus permitting the compiler to produce better code. Again, some Lisp systems, such as Franz Lisp (Wilensky 1984) have pursued a similar policy with respect to declarations.

A more complete description of the differences between conventional APL and the language accepted by the APL compiler is presented in the first appendix.

1.1. APL Terminology

One source of confusion between the APL community and the programming languages community at large is the fact that the language APL has assigned different meanings to some technical terms and also has introduced new terms not commonly known or used in descriptions of other programming languages. Thus, discussions of APL are often confusing to individuals who are not familiar with the language.

An *array* is a potentially multidimensional, rectilinear collection of homogeneously typed values; that is, an array can be a matrix of numeric values, or of character values, but not both. The number of dimensions in any array is called the *rank* of the array. An array of rank 1 (that is, dimension one) is called a *vector*. A *scalar* quantity is considered to be an array of rank 0.

Functions in APL, including user defined functions, have either zero, one or two arguments; and are referred to as *niladic*, *monadic* or *dyadic*, respectively. For reasons we describe in Appendix 1, in the initial version of the APL compiler we do not permit the user to create niladic functions.

The term *primitive scalar function* may be unfamiliar to non-APL users. Dyadic primitive scalar functions correspond largely to the type of operations commonly found in other general purpose programming languages, such as arithmetic functions, logical or relational operations. A list of the dyadic scalar functions is given in Figure 1.1. APL has generalized these functions to apply to multidimensional arrays in a pointwise fashion between corresponding elements. For example,

$$\begin{matrix}1 & 2 & 3\\4 & 5 & 6\\7 & 8 & 9\end{matrix} \quad + \quad \begin{matrix}7 & 4 & 1\\8 & 5 & 2\\9 & 6 & 3\end{matrix} \quad = \quad \begin{matrix}8 & 6 & 4\\12 & 10 & 8\\16 & 14 & 12\end{matrix}$$

There are also monadic scalar functions. In Chapter 5, the question of whether a dyadic primitive scalar function has an identity element will be important in determining the type of code that we will generate. So that we can later refer to this information, we have included a list of identity values for each function in Figure 1.1.

Whereas other programming languages may refer to the addition function as an *operator*, APL has defined this term in a much more restricted fashion. An operator in APL is a constructor used to build functions that extend the scope or purpose of a primitive dyadic scalar function in a special way. An example of an operator is *reduction*, which takes a primitive scalar function and extends it by placing it between elements of an array along some dimension. For example, if A is the two dimensional array,

$$\begin{matrix}1 & 2 & 3\\4 & 5 & 6\\7 & 8 & 9\end{matrix}$$

the plus reduction (written as +/A) is the vector of row-sums for A:

$$\begin{matrix}1 & + & 2 & + & 3\\4 & + & 5 & + & 6\\7 & + & 8 & + & 9\end{matrix} \quad = \quad \begin{matrix}6\\15\\24\end{matrix}$$

symbol	function	identity
+	addition	0
−	subtraction	0
×	multiplication	1
÷	division	1
*	exponentiation	1
∣	residue	0
⍟	logarithm	*none*
○	circular (trigonometric)	*none*
∨	boolean or	0
∧	boolean and	1
⍱	not-or	*none*
⍲	not-and	*none*
!	combinations	1
⌈	ceiling	minimum number
⌊	floor	maximum number
>	greater than	*none*
≥	greater than or equal	*none*
<	less than	*none*
≤	less than or equal	*none*
=	equal	1
≠	not equal	0

Figure 1.1: The APL Primitive Scalar Functions

In addition to reduction, other operators are scan, inner product, and outer product. For a more detailed description of APL there are any number of good textbooks, for example, (Gilman and Rose 1976) or (Polivka and Pakin 1975).

1.2. The Disadvantages of a Compiler

It would be dishonest not to point out that in certain circumstances there are advantages of an interpreter that cannot be matched by a compiler. Most fundamentally, a compiler is just one of many steps between conception and execution of a program, a path frequently riddled with loops and false starts. The phrase "debug/execute cycle" is often used to describe the typical programming process, in which the programmer makes numerous changes to a program before the final product is realized. An interpreter can minimize the number of operations required between iterations in this cycle and thus can make the program development process faster. With a compiler the time between successive iterations of this cycle is typically much longer, and thus the program development process advances much more slowly.

Similarly, many APL systems provide a pleasant programming environment, offering such features as the automatic retention of functions and data between computer sessions. This is difficult to duplicate using a pure compiler. Various combined compiler/interpreter systems have been constructed for both APL and LISP that try to minimize this problem. They retain the interpreter and the nice interpretative environment but permit the user to compile certain functions selectively into machine code for greater execution speed. While providing many of the advantages of both techniques, the major disadvantage of this method is that it requires the large run-time system (including the interpreter) to be present during execution.

As we have already noted, we were interested first and foremost in the quality of code we could generate. Thus, our programming "environment" is a rather primitive batch-style system; the programmer submits an APL program to the compiler, which generates an equivalent C program. This C program is then, in turn, passed to the C compiler, which generates the final executable file. This is not to say that our techniques could not be embedded in a better programming environment, merely that we have not done so.

1.3. The Compiler Passes

One advantage of a compiler over an interpreter is that the user is usually not overly concerned with the size of a compiler, whereas an interpreter must coexist with the user's data at run time and must therefore be as small as possible. This freedom permits one to consider somewhat costly operations, such as dataflow analysis, that would probably not be possible in an interpreter.

The APL compiler is structured in a conventional fashion, as a number of different passes. The intermediate form used to communicate between the passes consists of a symbol table and an extended abstract syntax tree, with the nodes of the syntax tree holding such information as the type, rank, and shape of the result that the function associated with the node will produce at run time. The following sections describe the purposes of each of the passes.

1.3.1. The Parsing Pass

While the syntax for APL expressions is so regular that it can almost be recognized by a finite state automaton, the addition of declarations complicated the grammar to a sufficient extent that more powerful tools were required. The parser for the APL compiler was therefore written using a conventional LALR parser generator. Since this parsing step is no different from parsers for more conventional languages, which are adequately described in the literature (such as Aho et al. 1986), we will not discuss it any further in this book. We note only that the intermediate representation used between the passes consists of a symbol table and an abstract syntax tree for each user function, and as the various passes operate, more fields in the syntax tree nodes are filled in.

1.3.2. The Inferencing Pass

The quality of code that can be generated by the APL compiler depends to a very great extent upon how much information can be obtained about the type, rank, and shape of the results that will be generated by expressions at run time. Much of this information is implicitly contained in a program, if only it can be discovered. The inferencing pass uses dataflow techniques in propagating information around the syntax tree. The algorithms used by this pass will be discussed in more detail in Chapter 2.

1.3.3. The Access Determination Pass

Chapter 3 describes the space efficient demand driven evaluation technique used by the APL compiler. This method requests values from an expression one element at a time, thus generating only those values that contribute to a final result. As we will see in Chapters 4 through 7, which describe the algorithms generated for the various APL functions, many optimizations can be performed if it is known that values for a result will be accessed in ravel (or sequential) order. This pass of the compiler merely marks those nodes that will be so processed.

1.3.4. The Resource Allocation Pass

In a conventional compiler, resources refer to objects, such as registers, that are usually limited in number and must therefore be shared. The APL compiler, on the other hand, generates code in a high-level language, C. In this context, resources refer to variables of various types in the generated code. Since there are no limits on the number of variables that can be declared in a C function, the resource allocation strategy is to give everybody whatever resources they require. This pass merely determines the number of resources that will be required by the algorithms generated in the final pass.

1.3.5. The Code Generation Pass

The code generation pass is the real heart of the APL compiler, and the principal feature that distinguishes the compiler from compilers for more conventional languages. The code generated by the APL compiler must be efficient in execution speed but must still be able to operate when types, ranks, and shapes are not known at compile time. Chapters 3 through 7 describe the algorithms used in the generated code produced by the APL compiler.

1.4. Compiling for a Vector Machine

APL is one of very few languages in which vectors and arrays appear as basic datatypes. Thus, the language would appear to be a natural match for those machines that have the ability to manipulate vectors of values in one instruction. Chapter 8 describes how the algorithms developed in the previous chapters might be modified or extended to make use of vector instructions.

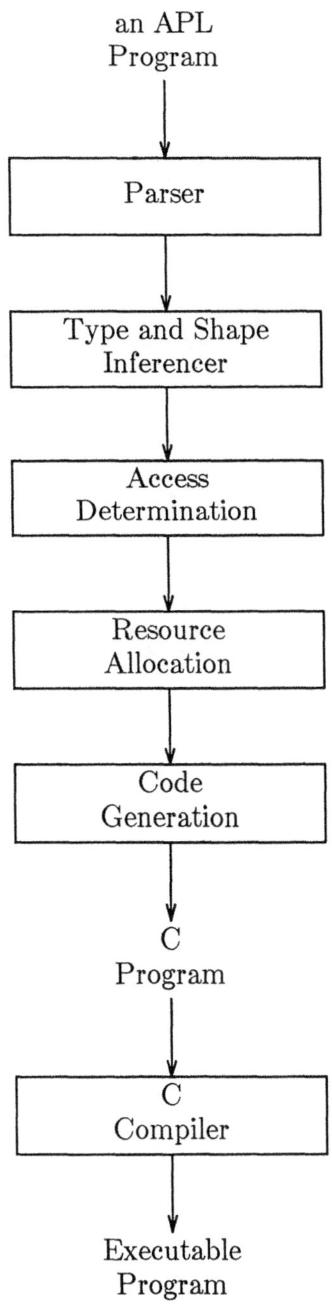
an APL
Program
Parser
Type and Shape
Inferencer
Access
Determination
Resource
Allocation
Code
Generation
C
Program
C
Compiler
Executable
Program

Chapter 2

The Inferencing Pass

Since conventional APL does not have declarations for identifier type and shape, and even in the language accepted by the APL compiler such declarations are optional, information concerning how a variable will be used must be inferred indirectly from an examination of the program text. Such information can be extremely beneficial. Consider the simple statement:

$$I \leftarrow I + 1$$

If the identifier I is known to be a scalar integer, considerably better code can be generated than if the program must be prepared to manipulate data of arbitrary type and shape (Wiedmann 1978). On the other hand, without such information the necessity of checking argument conformability prior to each primitive function can be one of the more time consuming tasks of an APL system. Thus, the ability to acquire information concerning variable usage is a critical factor in the success of an APL implementation. One of the most efficient means of obtaining this information is by means of dataflow analysis.

The dataflow algorithms described in this chapter produce information on two attributes of interest in code generation, expression *type* and expression *shape*. The latter can be further subdivided into *rank* and *size*. Although these attributes are distinct, the methods used to obtain information about them are similar and the gathering of information about both attributes can be performed in parallel. Information that could be obtained by other dataflow techniques and might be of interest to the compiler writer, such as live-dead analysis, or use-def chaining (Aho et al. 1986) are not considered here. Although other dataflow algorithms have been described in the literature (see the references for pointers to some of the papers), the algorithms given here are shorter, simpler, and tailored more directly to the language accepted by the APL Compiler.

For the purpose of explaining the dataflow algorithms described here, two differences between standard APL and the language accepted by the APL compiler are important. The first change involves the introduction of declarations. In remaining as close as possible to the APL spirit, the only necessary declarations are for global variables and for functions. This is the minimal amount of information necessary for the parser to distinguish the nature of every token at compile time. Although ambiguities concerning whether an identifier is a function or a variable are not common in APL programs, it is possible to construct examples where such a determination cannot be made at compile time without the use of declarations.[1] More extensive declarations of variable types and/or ranks are permitted and, if provided, give hints to the compiler that may result in the generation of better code. An example of this is discussed in a later section.

A second, and more fundamental, change to the language involves the elimination of dynamic scoping in favor of a two level static scoping. In this scheme variables are either local, in which case they can only be accessed or modified in the procedure in which they appear, or global, in which case they can be accessed or modified in any procedure. Dynamic scoping prevents one from, in

1. Similarly, it is also necessary to rule out niladic functions or to require declarations of function valence. Consider **F G expr**, for example, where expr is an expression and F and G are known to be functions; Either F is niladic and G dyadic, or both F and G are monadic functions. As we explain in more detail in Appendix 1, we were faced with a choice of either requiring declarations of valence as well as function names, or of disallowing niladic functions. In the APL compiler we chose to disallow the use of niladic functions.

general, establishing at compile time a definite link between a variable reference and a variable instance. Thus, it is much more difficult to discover information profitably about variable usage by a static examination of the code. Dataflow algorithms that work in a dynamically scoped environment tend to be both more complex and less effective than the algorithms presented here.

On the other hand, there are important characteristics of the language APL that simplify the task of dataflow analysis. For example, APL statements are unusually rich and complex. It is quite sensible to discuss analysis of individual APL statements in isolation for the purpose of discovering type and shape information, independent of any further intra– or inter–procedural analysis. This is in contrast to many other languages in which, for example, the average statement may involve one or fewer operations (Knuth 1971). Also, APL programs tend to be quite short, and thus an algorithm that has asymptotically poor running time, say $O(n^3)$, where n is the number of lines in a function, may be quite reasonable when the average function contains ten or fewer lines.

2.1. A Hierarchy of Attributes

We start by describing a hierarchy of classifications for the attributes of interest, namely shape and type. As we have already noted, in the language accepted by the APL compiler the user is allowed to provide optional declarations of variable attributes. Although declarations are not part of standard APL, the intent is to aid the code generator in the task of producing efficient code, while still providing the full generality of APL. The result is that attributes can be of two varieties, namely declared attributes (attributes the user has explicitly declared to be valid) and inferred attributes (attributes inferred by the dataflow algorithm from analysis of the code). Pragmatically speaking, the only difference between an identifier that has been declared to possess certain attributes and one not declared is the initial values given to the identifier attributes before analysis begins. A later pass in the compiler insures that declared attributes are not violated, which may necessitate producing run time checks.

A partial ordering of the attribute *type* is shown in Figure 2.1. The attribute *undefined* is given to undeclared local variables prior to their first assignment; thereafter, all expressions should be given one of the other attributes. In APL the type *boolean* refers to the integers 0 and 1, and thus the attribute *integer* is a generalization of boolean. The attribute *any* is given to an expression that can potentially produce a result of any type.

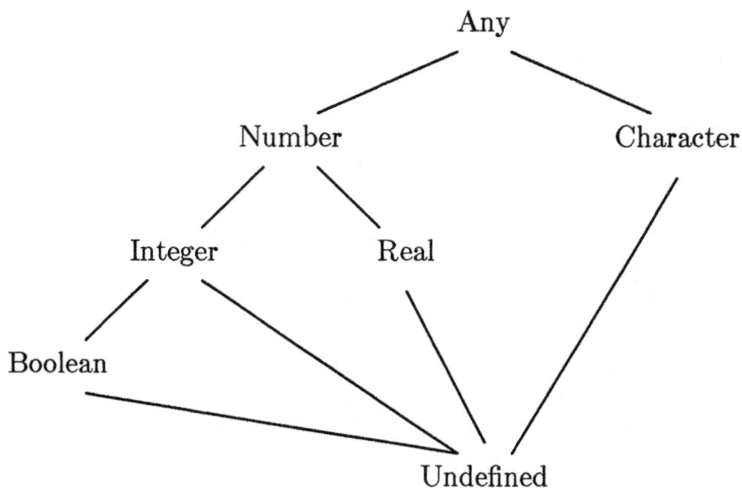

Figure 2.1: Partial Ordering for Attribute *Type*

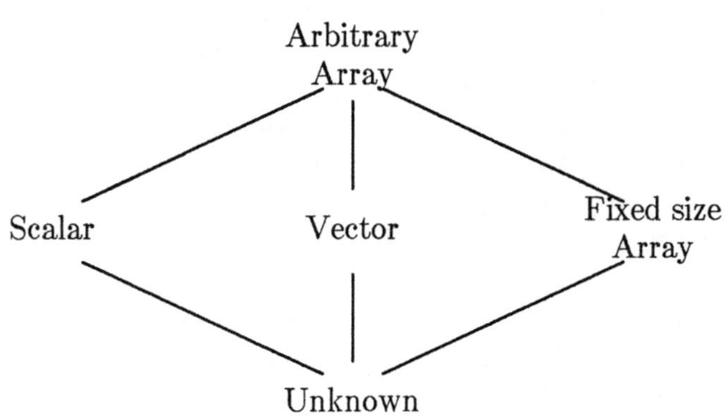

Figure 2.2: Partial Ordering for Attribute *Shape*

A similar partial ordering for the attribute *shape* is given in Figure 2.2. The attribute *unknown* is analogous to *undefined* for type. This is certainly not the only hierarchy that could be proposed. For example, one could argue that shape *scalar* should be considered to be a special case of shape *vector*. Experience with the code generator indicated, however, that whereas the special cases for scalar and vector were extremely important, code that was general enough to work for *both* scalars and vectors was seldom much smaller or faster than the code required to handle the general case. Thus, the given hierarchy represents a pragmatic description of the most important categories. Similarly, experience with the code generator indicates that very little is gained by exact knowledge of an expression rank if the rank is greater than 1 (that is, other than a scalar or a vector). Therefore, the decision was made not to permit declarations of rank other than for scalars and vectors. Nevertheless, information obtained during dataflow analysis concerning expression rank can be useful in predicting later scalar or vector shapes. For this reason inferred information concerning array ranks and shapes is preserved, when available.

The dataflow algorithms described here can be divided into three parts. The first algorithm is concerned with the analysis and propagation of information within a single statement. On the next level an algorithm is presented for the analysis of attributes within a single function. Finally, a third algorithm is used for the analysis and propagation of information between functions. These parts will be described separately in the following sections.

2.2. Expression Flow Analysis

The initial pass of the APL compiler transforms an APL expression into an abstract syntax tree. The dataflow analysis algorithms then operate on this tree representation to propagate type and rank information. To do this, the tree is traversed bottom up, inferences moving from the leaves into the interior nodes. For the leaf nodes, information is given by other sources: for example, constants have a fixed type and size; variables and functions may have been declared; or information may have been inferred from previous statements (see next section). Associated with each function is an algorithm for determining the resulting type and shape, assuming the type and shape of the arguments are known. For many functions this information can be codified as a table. For example, Figure 2.3 gives the shape transformation matrix for the binary plus operation. Figure 2.4 gives a similar matrix for type. In both cases the column index is given by the left argument and the row index by the right argument. By maintaining the distinction between declared and inferred attributes, it is possible to perform some compatibility type checking at compile time.

+	scalar	vector	array	unknown
scalar	scalar	vector	array	unknown
vector	vector	vector[1]	error[3]	unknown[2]
array	array	error[3]	array	unknown[2]
unknown	unknown	unknown[2]	unknown[2]	unknown[2]

Notes:
1. Can check conformability at compile time
2. Must check conformability at run time
3. Can issue conformability error immediately

Figure 2.3: Shape Inference Figure for Binary Plus Operation

Figure 2.5 illustrates how shape and type information can be propagated through an expression tree. The tree in this instance represents the idiom (Perlis and Rugaber 1979) for computing the number of primes less than a given quantity (in this case 200). Appendix 2 describes the code generated for this expression.

+	boolean	int	real	num	char	any
boolean	int	int	real	num	error	any
int	int	int	real	num	error	any
real	real	real	real	num	error	any
num	num	num	num	num	error	any
char	error	error	error	error	error	error
any	any	any	any	any	error	any

Figure 2.4: Type inference table for plus operation

function	type	rank and shape
A ←	integer	scalar
+/	integer	scalar
2 =	boolean	vector 200
+⌿	integer	vector 200
0 =	boolean	array 200 200
∘.|	integer	array 200 200
ι 200	integer	vector 200
200	integer	scalar

Figure 2.5: Propagated information for the expression
A ← +/ 2 =+⌿0 =(ι 200) ∘.| ι 200

2.3. Intraprocedural Dataflow Analysis

The control flow graph for an APL function can be represented as a sequence of expressions linked by directed arcs, signifying possible control transfer (Figure 2.6). In standard APL, every statement could potentially be the target of a goto arrow, however, newer programming practices have tended to limit transfer to statements possessing a designated label. The APL compiler insists that all transfers are to a labelled statement. There is a natural linear ordering for statements given by the order in which they appear in the program text, and this permits us to refer to "forward" branches and "backward" branches. Unlike more structured languages, we are not in general guaranteed that a control flow graph for an APL function will possess any nice properties, such as being reducible (Muchnick and Jones 1981). Thus, many conventional dataflow algorithms are not generally applicable. The algorithm presented in this section makes no assumptions concerning the topology of the control flow graph.

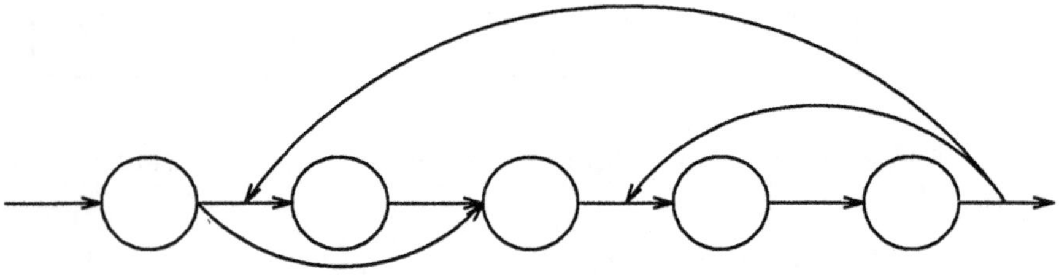

Figure 2.6: A Typical Control Flow Graph

We associate with each node in the control flow graph a list, called an identifier attribute list. This list records, for each identifier used in the function, the most general attributes observed for that identifier at the given location. There is also one such list maintained for the "current environment" as the algorithm steps through the function. We can say that one attribute list is *more general* than a second if *any* identifier in the first has a more general attribute than the corresponding identifier in the second list, regardless of the relationships among the remaining identifiers. Similarly, we can define a merge operation that takes two lists and forms a new list by selecting, for each identifier, the most general attributes from either list.

Given the conventional APL dynamic scoping rule, there is, in general, no guarantee that a local variable possessing some attributes prior to a function call will still possess those attributes following the function return. By discarding dynamic scoping in favor of a two-level static scoping, we eliminate this problem and greatly facilitate the gathering of information about variable attributes.

Having defined an identifier attribute list, the dataflow algorithm can be described as follows:

step 0 Initialize all identifier attribute lists to Undefined-Unknown. In the current environment list initialize globals and functions to Any-Arbitrary Array, unless other declarations have been provided. Initialize all other declared identifiers as per their declarations.
Set i = 1.

step 1 If i > number of nodes, quit.
Otherwise, merge the current environment attribute list and the identifier attribute list for node i, updating both lists to the merged result.
Perform the expression dataflow analysis described in the last section on node i, updating the current environment attribute list if appropriate (that is, if any identifiers are modified).
If node i is a branching expression, go to step 2, otherwise let i = i + 1 and go to step 1.

step 2 Order the list of potential branch targets. For each potential branch target, update the identifier attribute list at the target node by merging it with the current environment.
Let j be the value of the first (that is, lowest numbered) backward branch target which was strictly less general than the current environment, set i = j and go to step 1.
Otherwise, if no backward branch satisfies the condition, set i = i + 1 and go to step 1.

The first observation to make is that this algorithm does, in fact, terminate. The only time i is decremented is in step 2, and that can only occur if at least one identifier has an attribute more general than the attribute recorded at the target node. Thus, the number of times a node is examined in step 1 is crudely bounded by the number of nodes (n) times the number of backward branches (b) times the number of identifiers (i) times the maximum depth of any attribute hierarchy. Since b can be no worse than n^2, this gives us a running time of $O(n^3 i)$. While not asymptotically impressive, in practice the number of backward branches is considerably less and the running time is quite acceptable.

The second, and more important, task is to prove that the algorithm is correct. We first note that unless certification can be provided by global dataflow analysis (see next section), the attributes of all global variables and functions are checked at run time each time they are used. Thus, the only possible source of error is from local variables. Assume, contrary to our proposition, that some execution sequence results in at least one local variable possessing an attribute at some node that is not proper (that is, not less general) for the attributes recorded for that node. Let us consider the node at which such an event first occurs.

We observe that the attributes of all identifiers defined in an expression are given completely by the attributes of objects corresponding to the leaves in the syntax tree for that expression. Furthermore, these leaves come in five varieties: constants, global variables or functions, input-quads, or local variables. The attributes of the first four types cannot be wrong, and thus the only possibility is that some local variable possesses an attribute that is incorrect.

There are then two cases. The first case is that the expression node that we are considering is the first node executed. However this is not possible, since any local variables in the first expression would be undefined and the compiler would have detected the possibility of a local variable that had not been defined being used in an expression. The alternative is that this is not the first expression being considered, in which case the local variable that caused the trouble was defined in a previous expression. The new variable, however, would then necessarily have to differ with the attributes of the earlier expression, which would contradict the assumption that this is the first time an improper variable has occurred.

Having discussed correctness, the next question is whether the results are optimal. Unfortunately, a fundamental problem is that, like almost all dataflow algorithms, this algorithm is based on a static analysis of potential control flow paths, which may not correspond to the set of actually realizable control flow paths. It is rather easy to construct an example in which an identifier is used in one way (say as an integer) in one part of a function and in a different way (say as a character) in another. By inserting a conditional branch from the first part to the second, even if the branch can never be taken, the dataflow analysis algorithm is forced to assume a more general category for the variable than is actually necessary.

One further difficulty with this algorithm is that it cannot be used to perform backward type inference (Miller 1979). For example, consider the code fragment shown in Figure 2.7. By noting that iota requires its argument to be a scalar integer, we can infer that the result produced in the first line should be of this type. We are not, however, thereby assured that the result *is* of this type. Therefore, conformability checking code must still be generated. Since the only effect is to have moved conformability checking code from the second line to the first, very little has been gained. Examination of the code generated by the APL compiler using the algorithms given in this chapter have revealed few instances in which backward inference would have been useful in generating more efficient code.

n ← *some expression*
m ← ι n

Figure 2.7: An Example Backward Inference

2.4. Interprocedural Dataflow Analysis

One difficulty with the algorithm presented in the last section is that it utilizes only information contained within a single procedure. Complicated programs will frequently consist largely of function calls. In the absence of declared attributes, the most abstract categories possible must be assumed for the results of a function call. One solution to this problem is to perform dataflow analysis on an entire collection of functions.

An interprocedural dataflow analysis algorithm can be constructed in a fashion similar to the intraprocedural dataflow analysis algorithm described in the last section. In the interprocedural case, nodes in the control flow graph correspond to functions, and directed arcs correspond to potential function calls. A function call is characterized as a pair of "branches," one transferring control to the called function, the second returning control to the calling function. An arbitrary linear ordering can be imposed, or some analysis performed, to produce an ordering that reduces the number of "backward" branches.

Once again, the two-level scoping system of the APL compiler simplifies the task of dataflow analysis. Since local variables are not a concern at this point, all identifiers are global and of the same scoping level. Connected with each node an identifier attribute list will record information on all global variables and functions. In place of performing expression dataflow analysis in step 1, intraprocedural dataflow analysis on an entire function is used. With these changes the same algorithm is used as in the intraprocedural case. Details of the arguments concerning termination and correctness also carry over and will not be repeated here.

One difficulty with this technique is that the inferred result attributes of a function call are given as the most abstract categories which include all observed results for the function. Thus, relationships between the argument and result types of a function may not be recognized. For example, a function may always return a value of the same shape as its arguments. This information could, of course, be of considerable use in code generation. To gather such information, however, requires an algorithm of considerably greater complexity.

2.5. An Example - The Spiral of Primes

Figure 2.8 shows a set of functions that, collectively, produce Ulam's "Spiral of Primes" (Perlis and Rugaber 1979). We will use these functions to illustrate the utility of the dataflow algorithms that we have presented in this chapter. In response to a prompt from the input quad (line 20), the user types a small integer, say, for example, 10. The function *spiral* then computes an N by N array of integer values, arranged so that they spiral outwards from the center, as in:

```
GLOBAL VAR N

∇ Z ← SPIRAL L
FUN COPIES, LINEAR
A ← ⍳ N × 2
C ← 4 | A COPIES ( | −\ A )
G ← ⌊ 0.5 + N ÷ 2
E ← L [ ; ( ¯1 + N × N ) ↑ C + 4 × 0 = C
Z ← ( 2 ρ N ) ρ ⍋ LINEAR 1 1 2 ⍉ ( 2 ρ G ) ∘.+ +\ 0 , E
∇

∇ C ← A COPIES B
C ← A [ +\ ( ⍳ +/B) ∊ ¯1 ↓ 1 + +\ 0 , B ]
∇

∇ X ← PRIMES A
S ← ×/ ρ A
X ←A ∊ ( 2 = +⌿0 = (⍳ S)  ∘.|  ⍳ S) / ⍳ S
∇

∇ Z ← LINEAR M
Z ← 1 + N ⊥ M − 1
∇

N ← ⎕
Y ← SPIRAL 2 4 ρ ¯1 0 1 0 0 1 0 ¯1
X ← PRIMES Y
⎕ ← ' *'[1 +X]
```

Figure 2.8: Functions for computing Ulam's Spiral of Primes

82	83	84	85	86	87	88	89	90	91
81	50	51	52	53	54	55	56	57	92
80	49	26	27	28	29	30	31	58	93
79	48	25	10	11	12	13	32	59	94
78	47	24	9	2	3	14	33	60	95
77	46	23	8	1	4	15	34	61	96
76	45	22	7	6	5	16	35	62	97
75	44	21	20	19	18	17	36	63	98
74	43	42	41	40	39	38	37	64	99
73	72	71	70	69	68	67	66	65	100

This array is passed to the function *primes*, which replaces each value that corresponds to a prime number with a 1, and each nonprime with a 0:

0	1	0	0	0	0	0	1	0	0
0	0	0	0	1	0	0	0	0	0
0	0	0	0	0	1	0	1	0	0
1	0	0	0	1	0	1	0	1	0
0	1	0	0	1	1	0	0	0	0
0	0	1	0	0	0	0	0	1	0
0	0	0	1	0	1	0	0	0	1
0	0	0	0	1	0	1	0	0	0
0	1	0	1	0	0	0	1	0	0
1	0	1	0	0	0	1	0	0	0

These values are then used to subscript into a constant array, in effect replacing every 1 point with a star. The resulting pattern exhibits unusual lines that no one has been able to explain:

```
 *     *
    *
     * *
*   * * *
 *  **
  *     *
   * *   *
    * *
 * *   *
* *   *
```

When presented to the APL compiler, these functions generate a total of 157 nodes in the abstract syntax tree that is the internal representation for APL functions inside the compiler. Of these 157, one of the attributes type, rank or shape is manifestly apparent for 34 nodes (Figure 2.9). This is either because the node represents a constant, for which all the attributes type, rank, and shape are known, or the function iota or grade-up, for which the attributes type and rank are known, or an equality test or other function for which the type is known.

Number of nodes in syntax tree for which attributes are known		
type is known	34	22%
rank is known	27	17%
shape is known	22	14%
at least one of the attributes type, rank or shape is known	34	22%

Figure 2.9: Attribute Information Prior to Analysis Beginning

2.5.1. Statement Analysis

Following simple expression flow analysis of each statement in isolation, there are several inferences that can be made. For example, we can determine that the result of the addition and the division in line 6 will be real, and that of the monadic function floor in the same line will be integer.

In statement 7, although we as yet know nothing about the variable C, we do know that the result of the comparison of 0 to C will yield boolean values; thus, the result of the multiplication of this value by the constant 4 will be integer.

In statement 8, although we cannot determine the type of the argument to the function *linear*, we do know it has rank 2. Similarly, we can determine that the value assigned to Z will be an integer array of rank 2.

In the function *copies* we may not know the size or shape of the argument B, but we do know that the iota function produces a vector; thus, the index expression for the subscript must be an integer vector. In contrast to our earlier remarks, this function does illustrate one situation in which backward inference might be useful. If we assume that the argument to iota must be an integer, then we are logically led to conclude that B must be a vector. Making this assumption (and without further confirmation we would still need to insert run time checks to insure its validity), we can then go on to conclude the type and rank of the expression to the right of the epsilon. While this example might argue in favor of some sort of backwards inference capability, we shall soon see that interprocedural analysis provides, in this particular case, all the information that we need.

Finally, it is not surprising, since it is similar to the expression we described earlier in this chapter, that we can determine the type and rank information for almost all the nodes in the second statement of the function *primes*, even without knowing that the variable S represents a scalar integer.

All total, we can discover information about at least one of the attributes type, rank or shape in 49% of the nodes in the abstract syntax trees for these functions. More comprehensive data is presented in Figure 2.10.

Number of nodes in syntax tree for which attributes are known		
type is known	68	43%
rank is known	68	43%
shape is known	39	25%
at least one of the attributes type, rank or shape is known	78	49%

Figure 2.10: Attribute Information Following Expression Flow Analysis

2.5.2. Intraprocedural Analysis

Intraprocedural analysis infers that the value assigned to the variable A in line 4 is an integer vector. Armed with this fact, we can tell a little more about the arguments passed to the function *copies*, but we still cannot determine any information about the results of the function call, and hence the values assigned to the variable C in line 5. Similarly, we know variable G is integer in line 6, but since we know nothing of E this helps only marginally in understanding statement 8.

Number of nodes in syntax tree for which attributes are known		
type is known	75	48%
rank is known	75	48%
shape is known	42	27%
at least one of the attributes type, rank or shape is known	83	53%

Figure 2.11: Attribute Information Following Intraprocedural Flow Analysis

Intraprocedural analysis helps not at all in understanding the function *copies*, since it has only one line. In *primes*, although we can determine the type and shape of the variable S as being a scalar integer, we already knew everything there was to learn about the second statement. The complete data following intraprocedural analysis is shown in Figure 2.11.

2.5.3. Interprocedural Analysis

With the knowledge that both the arguments A and B in the function *copies* are integer vectors, we can determine that the result is integer and vector as well. Armed with this fact, plus the knowledge that the argument L to the function *spiral* is an integer array of rank 2, we can determine that E in line 7 is also an integer array of rank 2.

We knew from intraprocedural analysis that the rank of the argument to the function *linear* was rank 2. Although information about the variable E now permits us to expand this from simply an array into an integer array, this is still not sufficient to determine anything about the result of this function.

Although we were aware from intraprocedural analysis that the result of the function *spiral*, in line 2, was an integer array of rank 2, prior to interprocedural analysis we did not propagate this fact into the argument A to the function *primes*. Now, armed with this fact, we know that not only is the result of that function of type boolean but also that it is, in fact, a boolean array of rank 2.

The data following interprocedural analysis is shown in Figure 2.12.

Number of nodes in syntax tree for which attributes are known		
type is known	117	75%
rank is known	116	74%
shape is known	42	27%
at least one of the attributes type, rank or shape is known	121	77%

Figure 2.12: Attribute Information Following Interprocedural Flow Analysis

2.5.4. The Importance of Declarations

This example can also be used to illustrate how the judicious use of declarations can dramatically improve the quality of code that can be generated by the APL compiler. The global variable N is assigned a value by the input quad in line 20. This being the case, we are unable to determine the type, rank, or shape of the value. If, however, we declare that N is a scalar integer, then a wealth of inferences become possible. For example, we can then determine that G in line 6 is a scalar integer. Similarly, we can finally determine something about the function *linear*, namely, that in line 18 it produces an integer vector.

Even without performing interprocedural analysis, adding this declaration results in an improvement of the generated code (Figure 2.13). With the addition of interprocedural analysis, some attribute can be discovered for almost 90% of all nodes in the

Number of nodes in syntax tree for which attributes are known		
type is known	89	57%
rank is known	94	60%
shape is known	58	40%
at least one of the attributes type, rank or shape is known	98	62%

Figure 2.13: Attribute Information Following Intraprocedural Flow Analysis With the Addition of a Declaration for Variable N

Number of nodes in syntax tree for which attributes are known		
type is known	133	85%
rank is known	137	87%
shape is known	59	38%
at least one of the attributes type, rank or shape is known	137	87%

Figure 2.14: Attribute Information Following Interprocedural Flow Analysis With the Addition of a Declaration for Variable N

syntax tree (Figure 2.14).

2.5.5. The Size of the Generated Programs

It is interesting to compare the size of the C programs generated by the APL compiler under various conditions. Figure 2.15 shows this information. The table lists both the number of lines and the number of tokens (symbols) in the programs. As more and more information becomes known, smaller and smaller programs can be generated. The code for the final case, interprocedural analysis with the addition of the declaration for variable N, is presented in Appendix 3.

program	lines	tokens
after expression flow analysis	683	2816
after intraprocedural analysis	674	2776
intraprocedural with declaration for N	641	2610
after interprocedural analysis	617	2477
interprocedural with declaration for N	578	2279

Figure 2.15: Size of Generated Programs

In a similar manner, as the code becomes smaller it also becomes faster. For large values of N, the execution time in all programs is almost completely dominated by quadratic algorithm used by the function *primes*. In order to get a fairer sense of the relative speed of the code generated under various conditions, we therefore execute these functions repeatedly for small values of N, rather than once for a large value. To do this, we replace the main program with the following:

```
∇ TIMEIT W
I ← 0
L: X ← ' *'[ 1 + primes spiral 2 4 ρ ¯1 0 1 0 0 1 0 ¯1 ]
I ← I + 1
→ L × ι I < W
∇

N ← 10
TIMEIT 10
```

The function *timeit* executes the spiral functions repeatedly a fixed number of times, in this case 10. Execution timings for each of these five functions are given in Figure 2.16. As you can see, the information gained by dataflow analysis permits the generation of code that is, in this case, more than one-third faster than the code that can be generated without such analysis.

program	time
after expression flow analysis	16.3 seconds
after intraprocedural analysis	15.8 seconds
intraprocedural with declaration for N	15.3 seconds
after interprocedural analysis	11.4 seconds
interprocedural with declaration for N	10.1 seconds

Figure 2.16: Execution Timings for Ulam Code

Chapter 3

Code Generation Overview

The task of the data inferencing pass is to determine, to as great an extent as possible, the type, rank, and shape of the results that will be produced by each function represented in the parse tree. Once this information has been gathered, it is the task of the code generator to translate the parse tree into an equivalent program in the target language (in this case, the language C) that will, when executed, produce the desired results.

Just as there are many different programs that could be written in APL to solve a given problem, there are many different programs in the target language that can be claimed to represent the same algorithm as that given by any particular APL program. There are two objectives used to select the type of program produced by the code generation pass; namely, the desire to make the target program as fast as possible and the desire to make it use as little memory as possible.

The speed objective is perhaps easiest to understand, and it is here that the type information and, to a lesser extent, the rank information gathered during dataflow analysis is important. Scalar instructions that correspond to basic operations in the target language, such as addition, tend to be type specific; an integer addition is a different operation from a floating point addition, for example. If the determination as to the type of an operation cannot be made at compile time, then the generated code must call upon a subroutine to perform the given operation. The subroutine, which by run time knows the types of the operands, can select the correct operation. The difference in execution time between a single operation (such as an integer addition) and a call on a runtime routine can be many orders of magnitude. Thus, the correct determination of types and the correct utilization of this information by the code generator can have a dramatic impact on execution speed.

Less obvious, but just as critical, is the objective of reducing space. Many APL expressions compute a result by first constructing a large intermediate quantity, such as a multidimensional array, and then compressing this value by reduction, compression, or subscription. Thus, even in cases in which neither the inputs nor the outputs of an expression are large, the intermediate values can be substantial. Most APL programmers have had the frustrating experience of writing routines that work while they are testing them on small values, but fail for lack of space as soon as they try them on the larger values they are really interested in. The code generated by the APL compiler attempts to avoid this problem by using a space efficient demand driven evaluation algorithm.

Using this scheme, quantities are computed only as they are needed, not before. Consider, for example, a simple expression such as

$$A \leftarrow B + C \times D$$

where B, C, and D are large multidimensional arrays. The conventional execution technique for this expression would first place the value $C \times D$ into a temporary location, call it T, and then compute the value of $B + T$, storing the result into A. Clearly, the overhead associated with this is as large as the maximum size of the arrays. The demand driven approach, on the other hand, will compute each element of the result one by one; that is, one element from B will be added to the product of one element from C and one element from D, and stored in one location in A. Then the next element will be computed, and so on, until all values have been assigned. In this way, the overhead is reduced to that of a single scalar value.

There are problems with the demand driven approach, not the least of which is the fact that it may alter the semantics of a program in subtle ways. Consider, for example, the following expression

$$0\ 1\ /\ 6\ 6 \div 0\ 2$$

The conventional approach would produce an error because 6 is being divided by 0. The demand driven approach, on the other hand, produces no such error because the result is never required, having been compressed out. Despite this, the space savings of the demand driven approach make the technique attractive.

3.1. Demand Driven Evaluation

To better understand the demand driven evaluation technique, consider first a system in which each node in a parse tree is represented by a small, independent automaton. The automata are connected by wires in a manner corresponding to the abstract syntax tree and communicate by sending messages to each other. However, only a small amount of information can be transmitted with each message. Figure 3.1 shows the automata structure for the expression

$$A \leftarrow +/\ B + C$$

The topmost automaton (the assignment) is told to begin. In order to produce a result, it must first determine how large a quantity will be produced by the right side, in order to know how much space to allocate to hold the result. Thus the first message is passed from the assignment automaton to the reduction node.

> (message from assignment to reduction) What is the type, rank, and shape of your result?

The reduction automaton, by itself, cannot determine this value. Therefore, its first task is to pass the message down to the scalar plus function, which in turn passes it to each of its arguments.[1]

---

1. In theory there is no reason why the two messages from the scalar plus cannot be passed in parallel. We will later address the question of ordering operations.

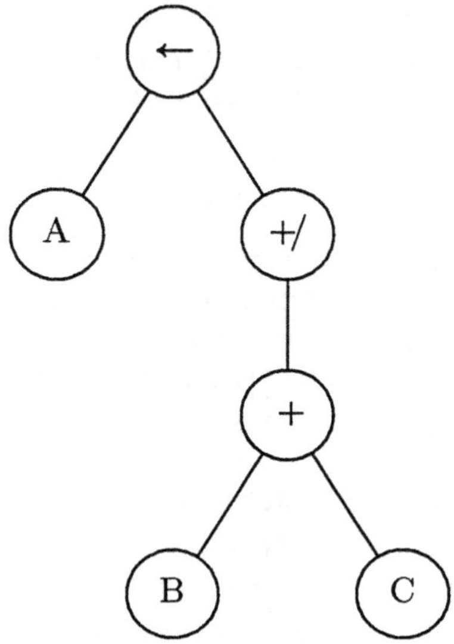

Figure 3.1: The syntax tree for A ← +/ B +C

> (message from reduction to scalar plus) What is the type, rank, and shape of your result?
>
> (message from scalar plus to identifier B) What is the type, rank, and shape of your result?
>
> (message from scalar plus to identifier C) What is the type, rank, and shape of your result?

Reaching the leaves, we are finally able to respond to a message without sending further requests. Assume we have the following responses:

> (reply from identifier B to scalar plus) My result is a scalar real.
>
> (reply from identifier C to scalar plus) My result is an integer array of rank 2, shape 6 7.

The plus automaton, having received these responses, first performs conformability checks to see if the arguments are legal in both type and size. It then determines the type and size of the result it will generate and passes this information back to the reduction automaton.

(reply from scalar plus to reduction) My result is a real array of rank 2, shape 6 7.

The reduction automaton checks that the plus operation is legal for arguments of this type and computes the type and size of the result it will produce.

(reply from reduction to assignment) My result is a real vector of size 6.

The assignment node finally knows how large the storage area must be to accommodate the result. It allocates this area and then starts to fill it in. It does this by requesting values one at a time:

(message from assignment to reduction) Give me the first value in the ravel ordering of your result.

In order to compute this value, the reduction node must compute the sum of the first row of the result generated by the scalar plus. It therefore sends a sequence of messages, processing the results as they are returned. (Note that the APL semantics require the sum to be computed in reverse order[2]).

(message from reduction to scalar plus) Give me the seventh value in the ravel ordering of your result.

(message from scalar plus to identifier B) Give me your value.

(message from scalar plus to identifier C) Give me the seventh value in the ravel ordering of your result.

(reply from identifier B to scalar plus) My value is 1.5.

(reply from identifier C to scalar plus) My value is 7.

(reply from scalar plus to reduction) My value is 8.5.

(message from reduction to scalar plus) Give me the sixth value in the ravel ordering of your result.

. . .

Having passed a sequence of messages to compute the values of the first through seventh elements in the result, and having taken their sum, the reduction node can finally respond to the assignment.

2. For a commutative function, such as plus, the result should be the same regardless of the order of evaluation. Later on, when we discuss the actual code generated for reduction, we will make use of this fact.

(reply from reduction to assignment) My value is 38.4.

The assignment stores the value in the appropriate location and then asks for the next value.

(message from assignment to reduction) Give me the second value in the ravel ordering of your result.

This continues until all the assigned values have been computed. Clearly, only those values are produced that are required for the final result, and the space requirements for intermediate results are minimized.

Note the similarity of this approach to that employed by object oriented languages such as Smalltalk.[3] Indeed, one could construct a working APL system in such a language in just this manner; however, the overhead of a general message passing protocol is considerably higher than is necessary in this case. This is because the number of messages required for the evaluation of APL is extremely small, and they are ordered in a very structured fashion. In this example, for instance, there were only two general types of messages:

1. What is your result type, rank, and shape?
2. What is the ith value of your result?

By utilizing this knowledge concerning the types of messages required for the evaluation of APL, we can achieve the effect of this demand driven approach with very little overhead. How this is accomplished is discussed in the next section.

3.2. Boxes

As we have just noted, the variety of messages necessary for the evaluation of APL is very limited. In fact, the two messages described in the last section are sufficient for all but a handful of functions.

The order in which these messages are passed is also very structured. A shape request will always be given *once* and be followed by some number of value requests.

Our interest, however, is in showing how the demand driven evaluation scheme can be rendered in programming code. In this light, it would be unacceptable if each of the value messages

3. For a description of the language Smalltalk see (Budd 1987).

required a separate section of code, particularly since, at compile time, we may not know how many times a value request will be needed. Instead, we modify the messages we will generate so that only one value request need be issued to generate an arbitrary element. The new messages can be described as follows:

1. Generate a section of code that will, when executed, return the type, rank, and shape of the values that you will produce. Respond with the locations that these values will occupy at run time.
2. Given a variable containing the index of a desired element in the ravel order of your result, generate a section of code that will, when executed, return this value. Respond with the name of the (internal) variable where this value will be stored.

For example, the assignment function generates code that, at an abstract level, can be described as follows:

```
{ code to generate type, rank, and shape of right side }
compute size of result and allocate storage
for offset =0 to (size of right side) − 1 do begin
    { code to generate element of result at index offset }
    store value in appropriate location
    end
release storage on old value of identifier
bind identifier name to new value
```

The name *offset* for the loop variable is indicative of the fact that the counter is really representing an offset into the ravel ordering of the result. Notice that the counter runs from 0 to the size minus 1; another way to think of this is that vectors in C are 0 based. The code sections in braces { · · · } correspond to the code generated by passing the appropriate messages to the right subexpression.

Another way to view the code generated by each APL function is as a template, or *box*, with holes in it.[4] The hole is filled by another box, corresponding to the arguments of the current function. That box may in turn have a hole in it that requires a third box, and so on until all the holes have been filled.

4. The term and analogy are due to Richard Lipton.

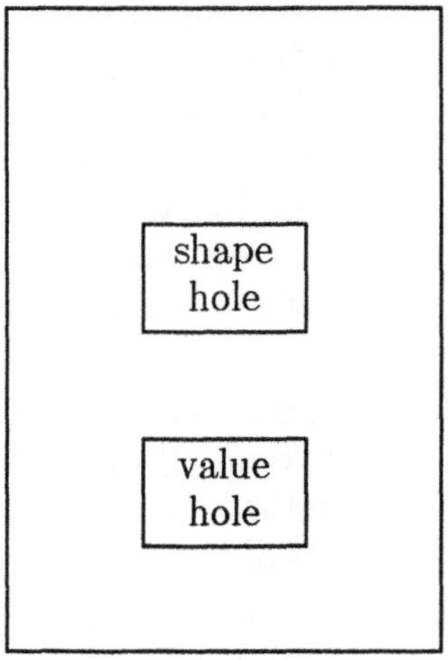

Each function has a box corresponding to the shape request (the code it will generate in response to the shape message) and a box corresponding to the value request (the code it will generate in response to values). By nesting the boxes one within each other, code can be generated for any APL expression.

Because some functions (compression and expansion, for example) require small intermediate buffers, which must at some point be freed, a third message is required to free up any temporary storage that may have been allocated. Thus, the sequence of messages for all APL functions, and the actions they induce, can be described as follows:[5]

1. Generate code to compute the type, rank, and shape of the result. In addition, if necessary, generate code to perform conformability checks on arguments. Also, if any temporary buffers are required, code is generated to allocate them. Finally, if any expressions can be computed here, rather than during the value step, code is generated to do so. This is because the normal expectation is that the shape code will be executed once each time that the expression is evaluated, whereas the value code may be executed many times.

---

5. The structural functions, to be considered in Chapter 6, require an additional message to compute the stepper value. The details of that computation are unimportant here.

2. Generate code to compute an arbitrary element from the result.
3. Generate code to free up any temporary storage that may have been required.

We can call the actions of a function in response to these three messages the three *phases* of code generation. Thus, we will often refer to code generated during the *shape phase*, code generated during the *value phase*, and code generated during the *finish phase.*

Note that, whereas for each function the order of phases may be very regular (first shape, then value, then finish), from a larger perspective things are not so ordered. A reshape function, for example, must compute the values of its left argument before it can determine the shape of the result it will produce. Thus during the shape phase of a reshape function, the left argument goes through both its shape and value phases. During the value phase of the reshape, only the value phase of the right argument is produced, and no code is generated by the left argument.

Advocates of attribute grammar parsing will note a slight similarity between the techniques used here and the methods used in attribute grammars (Waite and Goos 1984). During the shape phase, the request can be viewed as an inherited attribute being passed down, and the location of the result as a synthesized attribute being passed back (with code generation being an incidental side effect). Similarly, during value phase, the name of the identifier that will contain the index of the desired element is an inherited attribute, and the location of the result is a synthesized attribute. While superficially the method is the same, there are a number of differences on the implementation level (such as the fact that attribute grammars do not, by themselves, impose any order on the phases) that make it difficult to implement the APL compiler in this manner.

3.3. When Not to Use Space Efficient Evaluation

Most of the time, the space efficient evaluation technique that we have been describing is the preferable method for producing a result. There are, however, exceptions. To see this, note that some operations (such as outer product or scan) access their argument values repeatedly in the course of producing their results. This by itself is not a problem; however, the composition of these functions may produce a situation in which the space efficient technique is no longer preferable.

Consider the scan function, for example. A single scan requires, in general, $O(n^2)$ evaluations of the subexpression being scanned, where n represents the number of elements in the subexpression. By itself this causes no problem, nor is there, in general, a more efficient approach [although in some cases commutative functions will permit an $O(n)$ technique]. Consider, however, the composition of two scan functions. In this case, following the space efficient technique would produce an $O(n^4)$ algorithm. Saving the values of the inner scan would yield a $O(n^2)$ algorithm, at the expense of $O(n)$ storage. Clearly, there is a time/space tradeoff that can be made here. For small arrays either technique would probably be acceptable. For large arrays either technique presents difficulties, and the question is which difficulty is worse.

The APL compiler resolves this question by choosing to save time over space. Strictly speaking, this is not a problem for the code generation pass at all. An earlier pass identifies situations in which the composition of time inefficient functions can potentially cause problems. If it finds such a situation, it inserts into the parse tree new nodes to assign the inner expressions to temporary variables, and the higher functions read from these variables. Thus, it is as if code for an expression such as

$$\cdots +\backslash +\backslash A$$

were written as

```
temp ← +\ A
 ··· +\ temp
```

Other functions causing similar problems are outer product and the left argument to dyadic rotation.

There is another situation in which it is debatable whether one should use the space efficient demand driven evaluation technique. When printing an array, most APLs uses the smallest amount of space necessary to display the results neatly. Thus, an array of 0 or 1 values might display as follows:

```
1 0 0 1
0 1 1 0
1 1 0 1
0 0 1 0
1 0 1 1
```

If one of the values in the array is neither a 0 nor a 1 but instead an integer value, the spacing of the entire output is adjusted accordingly:

```
1    0    0    1
0    1    1    0
1 1437    0    1
0    0    1    0
1    0    1    1
```

To do this requires that the system save the entire array of values to be output in a temporary location, and compute the maximum size of any element prior to printing the first value. In keeping with our space efficient philosophy, we have decided instead to print values as they are computed, with no buffering. (The algorithm for output quad is given in more detail in the next chapter.) Since we do not know ahead of time the spacing that will be required, we use the printing precision and printing width system variables to determine the amount of space that will be occupied by any value. While this is admittedly a violation of the usual APL practice, it is in keeping with our space efficient philosophy.

3.4. A Note on Notation

The algorithms described in the next four chapters present the code generated by the APL compiler in a form of high level pseudo code. Although the actual code produced by the APL compiler is in a high-level language, namely C, many readers find C terse to the point of being cryptic.[6] For this reason, an alternative pseudo code is used. The appendices give examples showing the actual C code produced by the compiler. It is useful to note that there are four types of quantities manipulated by the generated code, which are described as follows:

---

6. Of course, one would not normally expect APL programmers to complain about a language being so terse as to be cryptic.

1. Scalar integer values. These are used to hold type and rank information, as well as maintaining loop variables and the like. These can also be used to hold boolean flags.
2. Result values. These are structures that can hold any of the three legal scalar types (integer, real, or character). Note that in C, as in APL, a boolean value is simply represented as either an integer 0 or 1. In some cases, if it can be determined at compile time what type will be produced by some subexpression, only one of the three fields of these structures will be referenced. If type cannot be determined at compile time, the entire structure is referenced by the code, thus permitting any of the three types to be used at run time.
3. Type / rank / shape values. These are structures used to maintain type, rank, and shape information, should it be required to be gathered in one place or maintained for a long period of time. For example, TRS structures are passed along with each argument in evaluating a user defined function.
4. Memory pointers. These are pointers that can point to any of the three scalar types (integer, real, or character).

Chapter 4

Simple Space Efficient Functions

The demand driven evaluation technique described in the last chapter works best with functions that are space efficient. In general, space efficient functions are characterized by the fact that individual elements of the result can be computed independently of each other, and the actions involved in this computation depend only upon the indices of the elements being computed, not upon the value of those elements. Not all APL functions are space efficient; however, the majority (and more importantly, the most commonly used functions) do possess this property.

In this chapter we describe the algorithms used in the generated code for some of the simpler space efficient functions. Algorithms used by more complicated space efficient functions are described in the following two chapters. In this chapter, we consider the following functions:

assignment, including nested assignment and assignment to quad
leaves, such as identifiers and constants
monadic and dyadic primitive scalar functions
reshape, ravel, and iota
outer product
subscripting

4.1. Assignment

The assignment function is notable for being one of only four functions that can appear at the top of a parse tree; the other three functions are assignment to quad, the branching arrow, and function call.[1] The last chapter described in broad terms the code generated for assignment. As we noted then, there are four tasks that the assignment function must perform:

1. Determine the type and size of the right expression.
2. Allocate storage for the values of the right side.
3. In a loop place values from the right side into the space allocated.
4. Rebind the identifier being assigned to the new values.

Note that rebinding the name to the new values is performed last, after all the values have been read. This is so that expressions such as

$$A \leftarrow A + 1$$

will perform as expected and not overwrite the old value before it has been used as part of the computation.

4.1.1. Nested Assignment

The algorithm presented in the last chapter assumed that the assignment function was the topmost function in an expression. This need not be the case, as an assignment can be used within an expression, for example:

$$A \leftarrow (1 + B \leftarrow \iota 7)$$

1. This is not to say that the user cannot write other expressions. However, the parser inserts an assignment to quad on top of any expression that is not itself an assignment, assignment to quad, branch arrow, or function call.

There are two separate algorithms used to implement nested assignment, depending upon whether the assignment function is accessed in a sequential fashion or not. Sequential access implies that all values are accessed once, in ravel order; no element is omitted, and no element is requested more than once. As we will see in following chapters, knowledge that an expression will be accessed in a sequential fashion often permits significant optimizations to be made. Note that the loop generated by topmost assignments always retrieves values in sequential order, and many functions will preserve this property.

If a nested assignment is accessed in a sequential manner, then no loop is generated. Instead, the loop generated by the higher functions is utilized.

Shape Phase

code to compute size of right side
allocate storage for result

Value Phase

compute the ith value of right side
store value in i^{th} location of allocated area

Finish Phase

Bind identifier to new values

It can happen that the assignment function is not accessed in sequential order. An example expression in which this occurs is

$$A \leftarrow ⍉ B \leftarrow 2\ 3\ \rho\ \iota\ 6$$

Here the loop generated by the assignment to A requests elements in a sequential fashion, but the transpose function is computing a new index value for each iteration of the loop, and these index values do not arrive in strictly sequential order. Since, in general, nonsequential access does not guarantee that every element of the result will be requested (a consequence of demand driven evaluation), it is necessary for the assignment function to generate its own loop to gather values. In this case the assignment is performed during the shape phase, exactly as if it were a topmost assignment in an expression. During the value phase results are then read out of the new identifier. Thus the effect is the same as it would be were the nested assignment removed from the expression

```
B ← 2 3 ρ ι 6
A ← ⍉B
```

Even if sequential access can be assured, it may also be necessary to generate a separate loop for an assignment if the value being assigned is subsequently used in the same expression. This occurs, for example, in the following expression:

```
B ← ( ⍉A ) +A ← 2 3 ρ ι 6
```

Finally, because a branching arrow may transfer control to another part of the program before the finish phase code has been executed, it is necessary to move assignment statements out of branch arrows, replacing

```
→L × ι ( A < B ← B +1 )
```

with

```
B ← B +1
→L × ι ( A < B )
```

4.1.2. Assignment to Quad

Assignment to box (quad) is similar to variable assignment, only the values are printed instead of stored. The only complicating factor concerns the proper insertion of newlines, so that 2 3 ρ ι 6 is printed as

```
1  2  3
4  5  6
```

instead of

```
1  2  3  4  5  6
```

This is accomplished by placing the following section of code after the portion of the program that prints each element. The effect will be to print a newline after each row, two newlines after each array, three newlines after each set of two dimensional arrays, and so on. The values s_i represent the shape of the result being printed, and n the rank of the result. The variable $offset$ is the index of the element being printed. The variable t is simply a temporary.

```
t = s_n
for i = n to 1 by −1 do
    if ((offset+1) mod t = 0) then begin
        print newline
        t = t×s_{i−1}
        end
    else break
```

Note that this algorithm differs from the one utilized in other APL systems, since the space to be used in printing each value is determined *a priori* before the first element is produced. As we noted in the last chapter, this is, however, in keeping with our space efficient philosophy in the APL compiler.

4.2. Leaves

Simple leaf nodes come in two varieties: identifiers and constants. Identifiers, in turn, may either correspond to variables in the user program or to internally generated storage locations. In any case, leaf functions can reply to requests for their shape or value without sending any further messages. If their type is known (as is always the case for constants), they can generate very efficient code.

Shape Phase

```
return the type, rank, and shape
of the constant or identifier
```

Value Phase

```
return the value of the constant or identifier
at position offset,
or if the constant or identifier is a scalar,
return the scalar value
```

4.2.1. Constants

The type, rank, and shape of a constant is aways known at compile time. All constants that explicitly appear in an APL function, as well as many other constants that arise during compilation (such as rank and shape values), are gathered together into a constant pool. During the shape phase, a response is merely a pointer to the rank and shape information for the constant. A pointer is also allocated during the shape phase and set to point to the values associated with this particular constant in the constant pool. Unless the constant is a scalar, during the value phase the value of the index for the desired element is added to this pointer, and the desired element is retrieved and returned. If the constant is a scalar, the offset is ignored and the scalar value is returned.

In the APL compiler a technique known as *lazy code generation* (Hanson 1983) is employed in an effort to produce smaller and faster programs. Using this scheme, the code for an expression such as a constant is not generated, that is, printed on the output, when the constant node is accessed in the value phase. Instead, the value phase code for the constant returns an *expression tree*, a simplified form of abstract syntax tree that can contain only scalar quantities and completely resolved array references. Some functions, notably the monadic and dyadic scalar functions, iota, and outer product, will produce larger expression trees from existing trees if the types of arguments and the type of the result is known. Various simple heuristics are used to simplify expression trees, for example, by adding constants together where possible. Functions higher in the parse tree then print out entire expression trees. In this manner relatively complex expressions can be constructed before any actual code is output for an expression. For example, in the code described in Appendix 2 the following C statement appears:

```
res11.i +=(0 ==((i6 +1) % (i5 +1)));
```

This statement includes code produced by two iota functions, a residue dyadic scalar function, the constant 0, a dyadic scalar test for equality, and a reduction operator. With the exception of the reduction, all these functions produced expression trees instead of code. The reduction operator finally traversed the tree to produce the code you see. Had lazy code generation not been used, many more lines of code would have been necessary. The examples shown in the appendices illustrate other instances of this optimization being employed to generate much more efficient C code.

4.2.2. Identifiers

In the internal representation of values used by the APL compiler identifiers consist of a structure, containing the following four fields:

1. The type of the identifier.
2. The rank of the identifier.
3. The shape of the identifier (a pointer to an integer vector of values).
4. The values of the identifier (a pointer to a vector of values, stored in ravel order).

During the shape phase it is sufficient to merely return pointers to the appropriate type, rank, and shape information. During the value phase the value field is indexed by the offset provided, and the appropriate element is returned. One complicating factor is that, if the identifier is a scalar (a fact that may not be known at compile time), the offset is ignored and the the scalar value is returned in response to all requests.

As we noted in the chapter on type and shape inferencing, early in the development of the APL compiler a simplification was decided upon that replaced the dynamic name scoping of APL in favor of a simple two-level name scoping. In this way, identifiers are either local (known only to the function in which they occur) or global (potentially known in all functions). One reason for this decision was the ease with which the two-level scoping could be implemented in the target language, C, since local and global variables could be mapped directly onto C local and global variables. This also resulted in a considerable simplification of the dataflow algorithms, as we have already noted in a previous chapter. In passing, we note that from the point of view of the code generator there is no fundamental reason why the conventional APL dynamic scoping could not have been preserved. To accomplish this, a search would have to be made during the shape phase for the appropriate binding of the identifier name. This would require a small amount of run time support, but basically all other features of the APL compiler (with the exception of dataflow analysis) would remain the same.

4.3. Primitive Scalar Functions

The scalar functions are the workhorses of the APL world. Not particularly flashy, nevertheless they do most of the real work in producing results. If the types of the arguments are known, many of the scalar functions can be implemented directly by operations in the target language. (Addition and subtraction are the canonical examples.) If it is possible, lazy code generation is used, and an expression tree is produced, rather than actual code. The sample output described in Appendix 2 shows a good example of a scalar function being combined with other functions in the final code. If the types of arguments are not known, or the operations are too complex, code is generated that will, at run time, call upon a subroutine to compute the result.

For monadic scalar functions the shape phase code merely returns the shape of the underlying argument, perhaps changing the type information. For dyadic scalar functions the shape code is more complicated, since one or the other of the arguments may be a scalar, and scalar extension must be applied.

The value phase code is simple for both monadic and dyadic scalar functions. The offset of the requested element is passed to the arguments, and the values they produce are noted. A new expression tree is then created that will, when executed, generate the desired results.

Note that scalar extension is facilitated by the fact that leaf nodes, such as constants and identifiers, will ignore the offset value during the value phase if they return a scalar. Thus, a dyadic scalar function node need not remember whether either of its arguments are scalar and can merely pass the same offset value to both.

4.4. Ravel, Reshape, and Iota

Using the demand driven space efficient technique, a few functions are almost free, in the sense that they generate very little code. Implementing ravel, for example, merely requires that during the shape phase the size of the right side is computed and returned as the extent of the vector result. Since the offset into the ravel ordering of the result is unchanged, no additional code is generated during the value phase.

Iota is almost as easy. During the shape phase the value of the right side is computed and stored as the size of the vector result. During the value phase the quantity in the index giving the requested position (plus the index origin) is returned as the value of the function. A compiler switch can be enabled to set the index origin to a fixed value (0 or 1), making this computation even faster. As we saw in the example C code cited earlier, when combined with lazy code generation, very efficient code can be produced.

Reshape computes the value of the left argument during the shape phase. It must also compute the size (number of elements) of the right argument. During the value phase it is only necessary to generate a single instruction. This one statement yields the remainder when the offset of the desired element is divided by the size of the right side, in effect causing elements from the right side to wrap around if there are fewer of them than requested. If we let $offset$ represent the index of the desired element and $offset'$ the index that will be passed to the right argument, this can be computed as

$$offset' = offset \textbf{ mod } \text{(size of right side)}$$

If it can be determined at compile time that the right argument has at least as many values as the result, even this instruction can be eliminated.

4.5. Outer Product

The value phase code for outer product is in many ways merely a variation on the value phase code for dyadic scalar functions. Instead of simply passing the offset for the requested elements down to the two argument expressions, new offsets are computed for both the right and left arguments.

$offset_{left} = offset$ **div** (size of right argument)
{ code to compute value of left argument }
$offset_{right} = offset$ **mod** (size of right argument)
{ code to compute value of right argument }
{ code to compute scalar function result }

This code, however, has the unfortunate property that the arguments from both subexpressions are requested once for each value of the result. As an example of how bad this can become, consider the sequential access of a large result. In this case, the left index would only change after the right subexpression had cycled through every element. If the left subexpression was the product of a complicated expression, the repeated construction of the same value from the left side could be quite costly. One alternative would be to buffer the left values, constructing a new value only if necessary. Code to accomplish this might look like the following:

$offset_{left} = offset$ **div** (size of right argument)
if ($offset_{left}$ <> last left offset) **then begin**
last left offset $= offset_{left}$
{ compute left argument at position $offset_{left}$ }
end
$offset_{right} = offset$ **mod** (size of right argument)
{ compute right argument at position $offset_{right}$ }
{ code to compute scalar function result }

However much an improvement in execution time this results in, for the case of sequential access we can do even better. On most machines the arithmetic operations of multiplication and division are considerably more costly, in terms of execution time, than the operations of addition and subtraction. Sometimes the difference may even be an order of magnitude. The optimization technique known as *reduction in strength* attempts to replace multiplications and divisions with additions and subtractions, using knowledge of how the replaced expressions will change as the loop in which they occur progresses.

In the case of sequential access of an outer product, we know the left offset will increase by one every time the right offset has cycled through all values whereupon the right offset will start over again at the beginning of its values. Thus, by properly initializing the value $offset_{right}$ in the shape phase, the following code can be used.

Shape Phase

$offset_{right} = 1 +$(size of right argument)
$offset_{left} = 0$

Value Phase

> **if** ($offset_{right} \geq$ (size of right argument)) **then begin**
> { compute left argument at position $offset_{left}$ }
> $offset_{left} = offset_{left} + 1$
> $offset_{right} = 0$
> **end**
> { compute right argument at position $offset_{right}$ }
> $offset_{right} = offset_{right} + 1$
> { code to compute scalar function result }

This code not only buffers the left argument, producing a new element only when required, but it also has eliminated both the division and the modular division previously required to compute the right and left offsets. It also continues the sequential access on into its left argument, thus potentially permitting further optimizations. We will see in subsequent chapters other instances in which the technique of reduction in strength can be applied in situations when results are generated in sequential order.

4.6. Subscripting

The operation of subscripting an expression by values generated from a number of index expressions is rather more complex in APL than in most other languages. Consider an expression such as

$$subscripted\ expression\ [\ index_1\ ;\ index_2\ ;\ \cdots\ ;\ index_n\ ]$$

For one thing, the size and shape of the result is not determined by the size of the subscripted expression but by the catenation of shapes of the index expressions. In fact, about the only constraint on the subscripted expression is that it must be of rank n, the number of index expressions. This is one of the few cases in APL in which constraints on the rank of an expression are imposed from above in the parse tree. (The dyadic form of rotation provides another example.)

The code generated for the subscripting operation divides naturally into two parts. The first part is, surprisingly, very similar to the code generated for the outer product. It is as if the semicolons in the index portion of the subscript acted as a sequence of outer products. In both cases an offset for the requested value is divided into two individual offsets for the left and right children.

In the case of subscripting, however, the left "child" is actually the combined set of subexpressions to the left of the current index. A temporary variable is used to hold the value of the requested offset as it is being manipulated by the index expressions, from right to left.

$temp = offset$

$offset_n = temp$ **mod** (size of index expression n)
$temp = temp$ **div** (size of index expression n)
{ compute value of index n at position $offset_n$ }

$offset_{n-1} = temp$ **mod** (size of index expression n—1)
$temp = temp$ **div** (size of index expression n—1)
{ compute value of index n—1 at position $offset_{n-1}$ }

. . .

$offset_1 = temp$
{ compute value of index 1 at position $offset_1$ }

The second part of the code then takes the result values computed for each of the index expressions and puts them together to form an index into the subscripted expression. Let s_n represent the extent of the nth dimension of the subscripted expression, and r_n the result value computed by the computation just given.

$offset' = r_1 - index\ origin$
$offset' = (offset' \times s_1) + (r_2 - index\ origin)$
. . .
$offset' = (offset' \times s_{n-1}) + (r_n - index\ origin)$
{ compute subscript expression at position $offset'$ }

If we know at compile time that the index origin is 0 or 1, then we can improve this code somewhat. For empty index expressions code is generated that is identical to that which would be generated for an iota vector of length s_n.

If desired, code can also be generated that will assure that each index value represents a valid subscript for the position in question, for example:

if ($r_1 < \textit{index origin}$) **or** ($r_1 > s_1$) **then**
issue error message
. . .

As with outer product, if we know the results are going to be accessed in sequential order, we can simplify the code for the first part, performing a reduction in strength to replace the two divisions (**mod** and **div**) with additions. The code generated for the first parts are then nested, one within the other, and new values are generated only when they are necessary.

Shape Phase

$offset_1 = 0$
$offset_2 =$ (size of index expression 2) $+1$
. . .
$offset_n =$ (size of index expression n) $+1$

Value Phase

if ($offset_n >$ (size of index expression n)) **then begin**
$offset_{n-1} = offset_{n-1} + 1$
{ subscripting code for index expression $n-1$ }
$offset_n = 0$
end
$offset_n = offset_n + 1$
{ compute value of index n at position $offset_n$ }

For the first (innermost) index expression the code is simply that code necessary to compute the value of the index expression at position $offset_1$.

If we were willing to compute the expansion vector (see next chapter) for the subscripted expression, we could in theory even replace the $n-1$ multiplications required in the second part with a single multiplication for each element generated. We have not done so, however, since our observations have been that most subscripted expressions have rank 2 or less, and thus this represents only marginal savings.

4.7. Mod and Div

Few machines have an explicit **mod** instruction, and thus most C compilers will translate the **mod** operation internally into a division and a multiplication. As can be seen from an examination of the algorithms presented in this chapter, we are often interested in both the quotient and remainder of a division of two values. In C we can compute these two results in one expression and thereby save one division operation. While this results in only a small savings, if it occurs inside a loop over the course of execution the results can be significant.

The single expression to compute both values is as follows:

$$\text{modresult} = \text{left} - \text{right} \times (\text{divresult} = \text{left} \div \text{right});$$

The examples given in Appendix 2 show this type of code being generated.

Chapter 5

Further Space Efficient Functions

In the last chapter we presented algorithms for some of the simple space efficient functions, such as the scalar functions and outer product. In this chapter we consider a larger class of space efficient functions, those for which the transformations on the indices can become more complex than the simple division that was required to implement outer product. In many of these functions, reduction for example, the determination of a single element of the result requires a loop to iterate over several elements of the argument subexpression.

In this chapter we describe the algorithms used in implementing the following eight functions:

reduction	scan
compression	expansion
catenation	dyadic rotation
inner product	decode

The next chapter considers a different set of functions that also have a space efficient implementation, although the details of that algorithm are quite different in nature from the algorithms described in this chapter.

Fundamental to the algorithms presented in this chapter is the ability to view a request for a single element as being given either by a single number, the offset of the desired element in the ravel order of the result, or as a vector representing the subscript indices of the element. The tool used to transform a request from one form to the other is the *expansion vector.*

5.1. Expansion Vectors

Consider an expression A of rank n. Let the vector $s_1, s_2, \cdots, s_n$ represent the shape of A (that is, the value of ρ A). The vector $e_1, e_2, \cdots, e_n$ defined by the recursive equations

$$e_n = 1 \tag{5.1}$$

$$e_i = s_{i+1} e_{i+1}$$

is called the *expansion vector*[1] for A. The value e_i is equal to the distance between adjacent elements along dimension i in the ravel ordering of A. Thus, the offset corresponding to position A[a_1 ; a_2 ; $\cdots$; a_n] can be computed as

$$offset = a_1 e_1 + a_2 e_2 + \cdots + a_n e_n \tag{5.2}$$

We will assume always that the indices are legal and zero based; that is, $0 \le a_i < s_i$. From this it follows that

$$\begin{aligned} a_{n-1} e_{n-1} + a_n e_n &< a_{n-1} e_{n-1} + s_n e_n \\ &= (a_{n-1} + 1) e_{n-1} \\ &\le s_{n-1} e_{n-1} \\ &= e_{n-2} \end{aligned}$$

Furthermore, in general

$$a_i e_i + \cdots + a_n e_n < s_i e_i = e_{i-1} \tag{5.3}$$

1. Some authors use the term *power vector.* There does not appear to be any standard terminology.

from which it follows that

$$(a_i e_i + \cdots + a_n e_n) \textbf{ mod } e_{i-1} = a_i e_i + \cdots + a_n e_n$$

From the definition it is clear that e_i equally divides e_j for all j < i, therefore

$$(a_1 e_1 + \cdots + a_i e_i) \textbf{ mod } e_i = 0$$

Observe that if x **mod** $y = 0$, then (xz) **mod** $y = 0$ and $(x+z)$ **mod** $y = z$ **mod** y. Using these we derive the following identity:

$$\begin{aligned} a_i e_i + \cdots + a_n e_n &= (a_i e_i + \cdots + a_n e_n) \textbf{ mod } e_{i-1} \\ &= (a_1 e_1 + \cdots + a_{i-1} e_{i-1} \\ &\qquad + a_i e_i + \cdots + a_n e_n\ ) \textbf{ mod } e_{i-1} \\ &= (a_1 e_1 + \cdots + a_n e_n) \textbf{ mod } e_{i-1} \\ &= offset \textbf{ mod } e_{i-1} \qquad (5.4) \end{aligned}$$

The converse identity, for sums of terms with indices starting at 1, uses the integer division function **div** . First we note a fact about **div** , namely, if x, y, and z are positive and y **mod** $z = 0$, then $(x + y)$ **div** z can be rewritten as $(x$ **div** $z) + (y$ **div** $z)$.

To derive our second identity, we divide both sides of (5.2) by e_i, giving

$$offset \textbf{ div } e_i = (a_1 e_1 + a_2 e_2 + \cdots + a_n e_n) \textbf{ div } e_i$$

We have already observed that

$$(a_1 e_1 + \cdots + a_i e_i) \textbf{ mod } e_i = 0$$

Under this condition it is safe to divide the right side into two parts, yielding

$$\begin{aligned} offset \textbf{ div } e_i &= (a_1 e_1 + a_2 e_2 + \cdots + a_i e_i) \textbf{ div } e_i \\ &\quad + (a_{i+1} e_{i+1} + \cdots + a_n e_n) \textbf{ div } e_i \end{aligned}$$

However, we know (5.3) that $a_{i+1} e_{i+1} + \cdots + a_n e_n < e_i$, therefore the right term must be 0. What remains is

$$offset \textbf{ div } e_i = (a_1 e_1 + a_2 e_2 + \cdots + a_i e_i) \textbf{ div } e_i \qquad (5.5)$$

If we multiply both sides by the value e_i, we obtain the desired identity:

$$(offset \textbf{ div } e_i)\ e_i = a_1e_1 + a_2e_2 + \cdots + a_ie_i \qquad (5.6)$$

Returning to (5.5), we next derive an expression that permits us to determine a_i from $offset$. Clearly a_ie_i **mod** $e_i = 0$, so (5.5) can be rewritten as

$$offset \textbf{ div } e_i = (a_1e_1 + \cdots + a_{i-1}e_{i-1}) \textbf{ div } e_i$$
$$+ (a_ie_i) \textbf{ div } e_i$$

Which, of course, simplifies to

$$offset \textbf{ div } e_i = (a_1e_1 + \cdots + a_{i-1}e_{i-1}) \textbf{ div } e_i$$
$$+ a_i$$

Since e_i divides e_j for all j < i, the division results in an integer, and it is not difficult to see that it must be a multiple of s_i (since s_i is a factor in e_{i-1} and all terms to the left). Therefore

$$(offset \textbf{ div } e_i) \textbf{ mod } s_i =$$
$$((a_1e_1 + \cdots + a_{i-1}e_{i-1}) \textbf{ div } e_i + a_i) \textbf{ mod } s_i$$
$$= a_i \textbf{ mod } s_i$$

However, since $a_i < s_i$, this yields

$$(offset \textbf{ div } e_i) \textbf{ mod } s_i = a_i \qquad (5.7)$$

As we will see often in this chapter, special cases occur at the endpoints. In the case of a_1, $offset$ **div** $e_i < s_i$, thus the formula for a_1 reduces to

$$a_1 = offset \textbf{ div } e_1$$

On the other hand, since $e_n = 1$, the formula for a_n can be simplified to

$$a_n = offset \textbf{ mod } s_n$$

The remainder of this chapter will show how these mathematical relations can be used to derive space efficient algorithms for various APL functions.

5.2. Code Generation for Reduction

Assume that we are computing an expression A of rank $n-1$, found by taking a reduction along the ith dimension of a second expression B of rank n (that is, using + for the reduction operator,

A = +/[i] B). Let e_k, $1 \leq k \leq n$ be the expansion vector for B. It is convenient in this particular instance to index the elements of A, as well as the expansion vector for A, by $1 \cdots (i-1),(i+1) \cdots n$. Let f_k be the expansion vector for A, and let s_i represent the shape of B along the dimension being reduced. It is clear that

$$e_k = f_k s_i, \quad k<i$$

$$e_i = f_{i-1}$$

$$e_k = f_k, \quad k>i$$

Consider the problem of generating the single element $A[a_1;a_2; \cdots a_{i-1};a_{i+1}; \cdots ;a_n]$. Let *offset* represent the position of this element. By (5.4) we have that

$$offset \ \mathbf{mod}\ f_{i-1} = a_{i+1} f_{i+1} + \cdots + a_n f_n$$

Using the relationships that we have observed between e and f, this is the same as

$$offset \ \mathbf{mod}\ e_i = a_{i+1} e_{i+1} + \cdots + a_n e_n$$

In order to compute the element at location *offset*, it is necessary to operate on an entire column of the subexpression B, namely, the column corresponding to

$$B[a_1;a_2; \cdots a_{i-1};\ x\ ;a_{i+1}; \cdots ;a_n]$$

where x ranges between 0 and s_i-1. According to the APL rules for associativity, this column must be examined in reverse order. Thus, the first element to be examined is

$$B[a_1;a_2; \cdots a_{i-1};\ (s_i-1)\ ;a_{i+1}; \cdots ;a_n]$$

Using the expansion vector for B, the position of this element can be determined as

$$offset' = a_1 e_1 + \cdots + a_{i-1} e_{i-1} + (s_i-1) e_i + a_{i+1} e_{i+1} + \cdots + a_n e_n$$

Using the relation between e and f that we derived earlier, this can be rewritten as

$$offset' = a_1 e_1 + \cdots + a_{i-1} e_{i-1} + (s_i-1) e_i + (offset \ \mathbf{mod}\ e_i)$$

We can factor s_i from the first part of the right side, giving

$$offset' = s_i(a_1 f_1 + \cdots + a_{i-1} f_{i-1}) + (s_i - 1)e_i + (offset \textbf{ mod } e_i)$$

but by (5.6) this is just

$$offset' = s_i(offset \textbf{ div } f_{i-1}) f_{i-1} + (s_i - 1)e_i + (offset \textbf{ mod } e_i)$$

Substituting e_i for f_{i-1} gives

$$offset' = (offset \textbf{ div } e_i)(e_i s_i) + (s_i - 1)e_i + (offset \textbf{ mod } e_i) \qquad (5.8)$$

Two special cases can be noted. When reduction occurs along the first dimension, $offset \textbf{ div } e_i = 0$, $e_i > offset$, and the formula simplifies to

$$offset' = (s_i - 1)e_i + offset$$

Similarly, when reduction occurs along the last dimension, $e_i = 1$, and thus the formula simplifies to

$$offset' = (1 + offset)s_i - 1$$

Thus, with these equations we can finally describe the code generated for the reduction operator. During the shape phase computations, the values of s_i and e_i are computed, in addition to determining the shape of the resulting expression. The values $e_i s_i$ and $(s_i - 1)e_i$ can be computed and stored in the variables t_1 and t_2, respectively. During the value phase it is desired to compute the element given by the variable *offset*, returning the result in the variable *result*. The code is similar to the following:

Shape Phase

s_i = shape of result along i^{th} dimension
e_i = expansion vector along i^{th} dimension
$t_1 = e_i \times s_i$
$t_2 = t_1 - e_i$

Value Phase

> $result$ = identity for function being reduced
> $offset' = (offset$ **div** $e_i) \times t_1 + t_2 + (offset$ **mod** $e_i)$
> **for** counter = 1 **to** s_i **do begin**
> { compute value of subexpression at $offset'$ }
> $result = value\ op\ result$
> $offset' = offset' - e_i$
> **end**

APL permits the user to perform a reduction using any primitive scalar function. Some functions, such as nand (not–and) or comparison, do not have an identity value (see Figure 1.1). For these functions the code just described clearly will not work[2]. An alternative algorithm gets around this problem by means of a boolean flag variable. The flag variable is set to **true** upon entrance to the value phase code, prior to entering the loop. As the first value is computed it is stored in the result variable and the flag is set to **false**. Thereafter values are combined with the previously computed result. If the flag variable is true following the loop, it means a reduction was attempted along an axis of zero length. Since the function being reduced does not have an identity, a domain error is reported.

---

2. To be precise, we require a right identity. That is we need an element y such that x op y is equal to x for all values x. Division, for example, has a right identity, namely 1, but no left identity. Residue, on the other hand, has a left identity, namely 0, but no right identity. Thus the algorithm presented here will not work for residue, and the alternative using a boolean variable must be generated.

```
flag = true
offset' = (offset div e_i)×t_1+t_2+(offset mod e_i)
for counter = 1 to s_i do begin
        { compute value of subexpression at offset' }
        if flag then begin
                flag = false
                result = value
                end
        else
                result = value op result
        offset' = offset' − e_i
        end
if flag then
        report a domain error
```

We note that the first alternative is preferable, when possible, not only because it is shorter but also because the *value* produced by the subexpression appears only once. As a consequence of the lazy code generation technique we described in the last chapter, this value can oftentimes be an entire expression, not just a simple variable. Rather than duplicating code for this expression, we would first store the *value* into a temporary variable and then use that variable in place of the *value*; that is, the code would appear as follows:

```
{ compute value of subexpression at offset' }
temp = value
if flag then begin
        flag = false
        result = temp
        end
else
        result = value op temp
```

We prefer not to generate the extra variable, the extra load and store on that variable, the extra tests on the flag variable, and the extra code if we do not need to.

We now present more efficient code that can be generated for the reduce operator under certain specific conditions. In each of these cases, modifications such as the one we have just described must be applied when the function being reduced lacks an identity value. We will not present these modifications since they should be clear to the reader.

If the object being reduced is known to be a vector, we can combine the offset computation and the loop.

> *result* =identity for operation
> **for** $offset' = s_i - 1$ **to** 0 **by** -1 **do begin**
> { compute value of subexpression at $offset'$ }
> *result* = *value op result*
> **end**

The code for the vector case is independent of the axis of the reduction (since, indeed, there can only be one axis). If the function with which the reduction is being performed is commutative, we can loop from 0 upwards, thereby making the subexpression have sequential access. Note that the property of being commutative implies that any identity must be both a right and left identity.

One more special case should be noted, since it occurs frequently enough and the improvement in execution speed is dramatic enough to warrant the extra effort. If the function being reduced is commutative (such as addition or multiplication), then we can move along the column of the subexpression in the forward direction, rather than in the backward direction. In general, this provides no savings, except in the case in which the expression will be accessed in a sequential fashion and the reduction is along the last dimension. In this case, the subexpression being reduced can also be accessed in a sequential fashion. This being the case, we can eliminate the computation of $offset'$ altogether by merely initializing it to 0 in the shape phase. The value phase code then becomes as follows:

Shape Phase

> s_i =shape of result along i^{th} dimension
> $offset' = 0$

Value Phase

result = identity for operation
for counter = 1 **to** s_i **do begin**
  { compute value of subexpression at $offset'$ }
  result = *result op value*
  $offset' = offset' + 1$
  end

5.3. Code Generation for Scan

For the scan operation, unlike reduce, the shape of the result is the same as the shape of the subexpression being scanned. Since the shapes are the same, the expansion vectors are also the same. Assume that we are generating code for an expression A of rank n, formed by taking the scan across the ith dimension of B, for example, A = +\[i] B. From the definition of the scan function it is clear that to compute a single element of A, such as

$$A[a_1;a_2;\cdots;a_n]$$

it is necessary to consider a section of a column of B, namely, those elements in the positions

$$B[a_1;\cdots;a_{i-1};x;a_{i+1}\cdots;a_n]$$

where x ranges between 0 and a_i. Here is one case in which the APL associativity rules, which require us to perform the operations in reverse order, are actually beneficial. The upper endpoint of the column is given by *offset*; we know each element in the column is a distance e_i from the next element, thus, it suffices to determine the number of elements in the column. This is given to us by a_i, which we know how to calculate from (5.7).

The code for the scan function can therefore be described as follows. During the shape phase computation, the values of s_i and e_i are computed and the shape of the resulting expression is determined. During the value phase it is desired to compute the element given by the variable *offset*, returning the result in the variable *result*. The code is similar to the following:

Shape Phase

s_i = shape of result along i^{th} dimension
e_i = expansion vector along i^{th} dimension

Value Phase

```
result = identity for function being scanned
a_i = (offset div e_i) mod s_i
offset' = offset
for counter = 1 to a_i do begin
    { compute value of subexpression at offset' }
    result = value op result
    offset' = offset' - e_i
    end
```

As with reduction, scan can be applied using a function that does not have an identity value. In this situation, the modification is similar to that used for reduction.

```
flag = true
a_i = (offset div e_i) mod s_i
offset' = offset
for counter = 1 to a_i do begin
    { compute value of subexpression at offset' }
    if flag then begin
        result = value
        flag = false
        end
    else
        result = value op result
    offset' = offset' - e_i
    end
```

Notice that, unlike the case for reduction, no value is required if the length along the axis being scanned is 0. As we did in the presentation of reduction, we will from now on assume that we are dealing with a function that does have an identity, with the understanding that similar modifications are necessary if this condition is not satisfied.

If the subexpression is known to be a vector, we can combine the counter and the computation of *offset'*:

Value Phase

```
result = identity for function being scanned
for offset' = offset to 1 by −1 do begin
    { compute value of subexpression at offset' }
    result = value op result
    end
```

As was the case with reduction, commutative functions provide the potential for a significant special case. If the function is commutative, the access is sequential, and the scanning is along the last dimension, then we can avoid having to build a loop at all. By keeping a counter, we can use the previously returned value to generate each new value, accessing the subexpression in sequential order as well. This counter is initialized to s_i during the shape phase. The generated code is then as follows:

Value Phase

```
{ compute the next value from the subexpression }
if counter ≥ s_i then begin
    result = value
    counter = 0
    end
else
    result = result op value
counter = counter + 1
```

Note that each new value of the result requires only one new element of the subexpression to be computed, so in place of an $O(n^2)$ process we can now compute the result in $O(n)$ steps.

If access is sequential, the function is commutative and possesses an identity, and the right argument is a vector, then we reach the ultimate in optimization:

Shape Phase

```
result = identity for function being scanned
```

Value Phase

{ compute the next value from the subexpression }
result = *result op value*

5.4. Compression and Expansion

The mathematical underpinnings for the algorithms used to generate code for the functions compression and expansion are very similar, and they are similar in fact to those used by the catenate function described in the next section. In both cases, the rank and shape of the result is the same as the rank and shape of the right argument, with the exception of the ith dimension, which is made smaller (in the case of compression) or larger (for expansion and catenate). Using the same notation as in previous sections, assume that we are computing some expression A that is formed by a compression or expansion along the ith dimension of some expression B. Let e_j represent the expansion vector for B and f_j, the expansion vector for A. Let s_i be the shape of A in the ith dimension, and s'_i the corresponding shape in B. We therefore have the following relations:

$$e_j = f_j, \quad j \geq i$$
$$e_j = (f_j \textbf{ div } s_i)\, s'_i, \quad j < i$$

Assume that we wish to compute a specific element from the result,

$$A[a_1;a_2; \cdots ;a_n]$$

Let $offset = a_1 f_1 + \cdots + a_n f_n$. To compute this value, it is necessary to determine a different value in the subexpression B. The indices for this value differ only in the ith dimension, so we can write it as

$$B[a_1; \cdots ;a_{i-1};a'_i;a_{i+1} \cdots a_n]$$

We postpone for the moment the discussion concerning how a'_i is computed (expansion and compression differ in this regard) and concentrate on computing the offset for this value as a function of a'_i.

Clearly, the offset for this position is

$$offset' = a_1 e_1 + \cdots + a'_i e_i + \cdots a_n e_n$$

Since the expansion vectors for A and B are the same beyond i, we can easily eliminate the later terms:

$$offset' = a_1 e_1 + \cdots + a'_i e_i + (offset \ \mathbf{mod}\ e_i)$$

We can factor out an s'_i term from the left side. If we then multiply the summation by s_i (at the same time dividing by s_i to retain balance), the e_j terms become f_j.

$$offset' = ((a_1 f_1 + \cdots + a_{i-1} f_{i-1})s'_i) \ \mathbf{div}\ s_i$$
$$+ a'_i e_i + (offset \ \mathbf{mod}\ e_i)$$

Applying (5.6) then gives us:

$$offset' = ((offset \ \mathbf{div}\ f_{i-1}) f_{i-1})s'_i) \ \mathbf{div}\ s_i$$
$$+ a'_i e_i + (offset \ \mathbf{mod}\ e_i)$$

However, as we observed previously, $(f_{i-1} \ \mathbf{div}\ s_i)s'_i$ is just e_{i-1}; thus, this can be simplified to

$$offset' = (offset \ \mathbf{div}\ f_{i-1})e_{i-1})$$
$$+ a'_i e_i + (offset \ \mathbf{mod}\ e_i)$$

Substituting $e_i s_i$ for f_{i-1} gives us

$$offset' = (offset \ \mathbf{div}\ (e_i s_i))e_{i-1})$$
$$+ a'_i e_i + (offset \ \mathbf{mod}\ e_i)$$

Rewriting e_{i-1} in terms of e_i and joining terms gives us our final form:

$$offset' = ((offset \ \mathbf{div}\ (e_i s_i))s'_i) + a'_i)e_i$$
$$+ (offset \ \mathbf{mod}\ e_i) \qquad (5.9)$$

There are the usual special cases for the first and last axis. For the first axis the **div** term disappears, leaving $a'_i e_i + offset \ \mathbf{mod}\ e_i$. For the last axis e_i is 1, thus simplifying the formula to $(offset \ \mathbf{div}\ s_i)s'_i + a'_i$. Finally, if at compile time we know that the right term is a vector, no calculation at all is needed, as $offset'=a'_i$.

Let us return to the question of how this can be used to generate code for the compression function. The first observation is that the rank and shape of a compressed expression is given by the rank and shape of the right subexpression, with the exception that the ith element of the shape is determined by the number of 1's in the left subexpression. Therefore, during the shape phase the left subexpression must be scanned to determine the number of 1 values. But we can do better, for we can compute at this point the offsets along the ith dimension that each entry will generate into the right subexpression. An example will help clarify this idea. Suppose we are computing the compression

A ← 0 1 0 1 0 1 1 0 /[i] B

As we scan the left, we note that there are four 1's; therefore, the resulting value will have shape 4 along the ith dimension. However, we can also build the vector 1 3 5 6, which tells us that the first column (with index 0) will be found by looking at the column with index 1 in B. The second column will be found by looking at the column with index 3, and so on.

The shape phase code for compression, therefore, looks similar to the following:

Shape Phase

```
{ allocate storage[3] for compression index vector v }
size = 0
for index = 0 to (size of left) − 1 do begin
    get left element x
    if (x = 1) then begin
        size = size + 1
        v[size] = index
        end
    end
```

In the end, the variable *size* indicates the number of 1 elements in the left subexpression and, therefore, the size along the ith dimension of the result.

During the value phase the first step is to use (5.7) to compute a_i, the ith value of the index for the desired element. This value is then used to index into the compression index vector constructed

3. Clearly it is only necessary to allocate enough storage to accommodate the number of 1 elements in the left argument. However, this number is not known at the time the storage must be allocated. An upper bound, however, is given by the size of the left argument, which is known at this point. Thus, the amount of storage requested is equal to the size of the argument.

during the shape phase, resulting in a new index a'_i. This value is then used in the formula derived earlier in this section, resulting in a new $offset'$, which is then passed to the right subexpression.

Value Phase

$a_i = (offset \textbf{ div } e_i) \textbf{ mod } s_i$
$a' = \mathrm{v}[a_i]$
$offset' = ((offset \textbf{ div } (e_i s_i))s'_i) + a')e_i + (offset \textbf{ mod } e_i)$
{ compute value at $offset'$ in the left argument }

The code for expansion is in many ways very similar. For expansion the size along the ith dimension is given by the number of elements in the left subexpression, not just the terms with value 1. In place of the compression index vector, the corresponding vector for expansion records whether the associated value is nonzero (say, by placing a negative 1 in the vector for 0 entries), and if it is nonzero, the offset to be used in the right side. During the value phase a_i is computed, as for compression, and used to index into this vector. If a negative value is found, the fill element for the type of the right side (either 0 or blank) is returned; otherwise, the computation is the same as for compression.

Value Phase

$a_i = (offset \textbf{ div } e_i) \textbf{ mod } s_i$
if $\mathrm{v}[a_i] < 0$ **then**
  result is fill
else begin
  $a' = \mathrm{v}[a_i]$
  $offset' = ((offset \textbf{ div } (e_i s_i))s'_i) + a')e_i$
    $+ (offset \textbf{ mod } e_i)$
  { compute value of the right argument at $offset'$ }
  end

If an expansion is accessed in sequential order and the axis is the last dimension, then the argument subexpression will also be accessed in sequential order. It is still necessary to compute a_i, but the computation of $offset'$ can be replaced by a simple increment, assuming it is initialized to 0 during the shape phase.

Value Phase

```
a_i = (offset div e_i) mod s_i
if v[a_i] < 0 then
    result is fill
else begin
    { compute value of right argument at offset' }
    offset' = offset' + 1
    end
```

5.5. Code Generation for Catenation

In principle, code generation for the catenation function is similar to, and no more difficult than, code generation for compression and expansion. In both cases the basic idea is to modify only one dimension of a request, forming a new request that is then passed on to a child. In practice, however, the code generation for catenation is complicated by a large number of special cases. Consider, for example, the computation of e_i, used by (5.7) to obtain the index along the ith dimension a_i. The following situations are all possible:

- The rank and shape of both subexpressions to the catenation are the same, except along the ith axis. In this case, e_i will be the same for both arguments, and thus either will suffice.
- The rank of the left subexpression is less than that of the right subexpression. (This is permitted if the left subexpression is a scalar, or if it matches the shape of the right subexpression in all but the ith dimension). In this case, the value e_i should be taken from the right subexpression.
- The converse of the previous case, that is the rank of the right subexpression is less than that of the left subexpression. In this case the value e_i should be taken from the left subexpression.

Let s_L be the size of the left subexpression in the ith dimension, or 1 if the rank of the left subexpression is less than the right subexpression. Similarly, let s_R be the size of the right subexpression, or 1 if the rank of the right subexpression is less than the left subexpression. The size of the result along the ith dimension will, therefore, be $s_L + s_R$. During the shape phase, code is generated to compute e_i, s_L, and s_R . Using these quantities, the value phase code can be described.

During the value phase, the first step is to compute a_i, using (5.7). This quantity is then compared to s_L. If it is less, the desired element is found in the left subexpression, otherwise the desired element will be found in the right subexpression. In either case, the same formula that was used in the compression code can be used to determine the offset into the subexpression.

Value Phase

$a_i = (offset \textbf{ div } e_i) \textbf{ mod } (s_L + s_R)$
if $a_i < s_L$ **then begin**
    $offset'_L = (offset \textbf{ div } (e_i(s_L + s_R))) \times s_L) + a_i) \times e_i$
        $+ (offset \textbf{ mod } e_i)$
    { compute value of left subexpression at $offset'_L$ }
    end
else begin
    $a_i = a_i - s_L$
    $offset'_R = (offset \textbf{ div } (e_i(s_L + s_R))) \times s_R) + a_i) \times e_i$
        $+ (offset \textbf{ mod } e_i)$
    { compute value of right subexpression at $offset'_R$ }
    end

As with most of the functions described in this chapter, if access to the results is sequential, then better code can be generated. Catenation is unique, however, in that this special case is applicable regardless of the axis along which the catenation takes place. All that is required is that $offset'_L$ and $offset'_R$ be initialized to 0 during the shape phase.

Value Phase

$a_i = (offset \textbf{ div } e_i) \textbf{ mod } (s_L + s_R)$
if $a_i < s_L$ **then begin**
    { compute value of left subexpression at $offset'_L$ }
    $offset'_L = offset'_L + 1$
    end
else begin
    { compute value of right subexpression at $offset'_R$ }
    $offset'_R = offset'_R + 1$
    end

5.6. Code Generation for Dyadic Rotation

For the dyadic rotation function, rank and shape of the result is the same as the rank and shape of the right argument. The left argument has rank one less, and must match the shape of the right except in the position being rotated around. Assume that we are computing an expression A =B ⌽ [i] C. Let e_i be the expansion vector for A (also for C) and f_i the expansion vector for B. Assume that we want to compute the element of A stored at a particular $offset$, and let the element be represented as $A[a_1; \cdots; a_n]$. The first step is to compute the element of B given by the same indices with the ith entry removed, that is $B[a_1; \cdots; a_{i-1}; a_{i+1}; \cdots; a_n]$. Clearly, this is given by:

$$offset' = a_1 f_1 + \cdots + a_{i-1} f_{i-1} + a_{i+1} f_{i+1} + \cdots + a_n f_n$$

As we have seen several times already (in reduction and scan, for example), we can replace the right side of the summation by $offset$ **mod** f_{i+1}, which is $offset$ **mod** e_i. If we multiply the left side of the summation by s_i, dividing out by the same value to retain balance, we can replace by f_i terms with e_i, yielding

$$offset' = (a_1 e_1 + \cdots + a_{i-1} e_{i-1}) \textbf{ div } s_i + (offset \textbf{ mod } e_i)$$

Applying (5.6) gives us the desired formula:

$$offset' = (offset \textbf{ div } (e_i s_i)) e_i + offset \textbf{ mod } e_i$$

As always, there are special cases for the first and last axis. In the former case, the first term disappears, leaving

$$offset' = offset \textbf{ mod } e_i$$

In the second case, e_i is 1, thereby reducing the computation to

$$offset' = offset \textbf{ div } s_i$$

This value is then used to index into the left argument, resulting in a value r. The desired element is found in the right argument at the position modified in the ith position by the value r. A complicating factor is that r may be either positive or negative, but the result value a'_i must be between 0 and s_i. To determine this, we first apply (5.7) to obtain a_i. The new value is then computed as follows:

$$a'_i = a_i + r$$
$$\textbf{if } a'_i < 0 \textbf{ then } a'_i = a'_i + s_i$$
$$\textbf{if } a'_i \geq s_i \textbf{ then } a'_i = a'_i - s_i$$

The computation of the correct value then follows closely the algorithm used in compression and expansion.

5.7. Inner Product and Decode

We describe the code for the general case of inner product. The special cases (one argument scalar or vector) necessitate variations on the general idea. In the general case, the last dimension of the left argument must match the first dimension of the right argument; that is, if we let $L_1, L_2, \cdots, L_n$ represent the size of the left argument, and $R_1, R_2, \cdots, R_m$ represent the size of the right argument, it must be true that $L_n = R_1$. The shape of the result is given by concatenating the shapes of the left and right arguments, deleting these two positions; that is, $L_1, L_2, \cdots, L_{n-1}, R_2, \cdots, R_m$.

As with outer product, the first step in computing an inner product is to convert a request for a specific element into a pair of requests for the right and left children. In the outer product this is accomplished by dividing the offset by the size of the right subexpression. In this case, we want the size of the right subexpression without the first dimension. This quantity is given by e_1, the first element of the expansion vector for the right side. Thus, if *index* is used to represent the position of a given element in the column being processed by the inner product, the position of the corresponding element in the right subexpression will be given by

$$offset'_R = offset \textbf{ mod } e_1 + index \times e_1$$

Since the index will decrease in an orderly fashion, most of this computation can be preprocessed before the loop begins, and a single subtraction can be used to compute each new offset.

On the left side, dividing by e_1 results in an offset into the left argument minus the first dimension. If we multiply this by L_n, the size of the first dimension, we obtain the offset for the beginning of the column that will be processed by the inner product. To obtain a specific element in the column, it is only necessary to add the index element.

$$offset'_L = (offset \textbf{ div } e_1)L_n + index$$

With these equations we can describe the code generated for the inner product. Note that the loop invariant code for the two computations has been moved out of the loop, and a reduction in strength has been applied. We present the code as though it were the matrix multiplication inner product +.×, although any scalar functions can be treated similarly. The shape phase is complicated by the fact that one or the other of the arguments may be a scalar.

Shape Phase

L = shape of right argument in first position
e_1 = expansion vector of right argument in first position
if (right argument is scalar) **then**
  L = shape of left argument in last position

Value Phase

$offset'_L = (offset \textbf{ div } e_1) \times L + (L-1)$
$offset'_R = offset \textbf{ mod } e_1 + (L-1) \times e_1$
result = identity for first function (+, for example)
for counter = $L-1$ **to** 0 **by** -1 **do begin**
  { compute $value_L$ of the left subexpression }
  { compute $value_R$ of the right subexpression }
  result = $value_L \times value_R$ + result
  $offset'_L = offset'_L - 1$
  $offset'_R = offset'_R - e_1$
  end

As with scan and reduction, this code is incorrect if the first function of the inner product fails to have an identity value. In this case, the code is modified as follows:

$offset'_L = (offset \text{ div } e_1) \times L + (L-1)$
$offset'_R = offset \text{ mod } e_1 + (L-1) \times e_1$
flag = **true**
for counter = $L-1$ **to** 0 **by** -1 **do begin**
  { compute $value_L$ of the left subexpression }
  { compute $value_R$ of the right subexpression }
  if flag **then begin**
    result = $value_L \times value_R$
    flag = **false**
    end
  else
    result = $value_L \times value_R$ + result
  $offset'_L = offset'_L - 1$
  $offset'_R = offset'_R - e_1$
  end

If either the left or right arguments are vector, then the computation of $offset'_L$ or $offset'_R$ can be eliminated, the value being replaced by the counter.

The generated code for decode is very similar to that generated for the matrix multiplication (+.×) inner product. In the case of decode, however, a temporary variable is maintained for the left side. This variable is used in the result calculation and then multiplied by the appropriate element in the left subexpression:

$offset'_L = (offset \text{ div } e_1) \times L + (L-1)$
$offset'_R = offset \text{ mod } e_1 + (L-1) \times e_1$
result = identity for addition (zero)
t = identity for multiplication (one)
for counter = $L-1$ **to** 0 **by** -1 **do begin**
  { compute $value_R$ of the right subexpression }
  result = $t \times value_R$ + result
  { compute $value_L$ of the left subexpression }
  $t = t \times value_L$
  $offset'_L = offset'_L - 1$
  $offset'_R = offset'_R - e_1$
  end

Chapter 6

Structural Functions

In this chapter we present algorithms that are used in implementing the following functions:

monadic transpose	dyadic transpose
take	drop
reversal	

These functions are only halfway space efficient, in the sense of Chapter 3. While they are all space efficient with regard to their right argument, those that use a left argument require the value of the left argument to be known before their shape can be determined. Thus, the entire left argument is collected and buffered into a temporary location during their shape phase. This temporary buffer is freed after all values have been requested.

These functions can be characterized by the fact that they modify positions of elements but not the values of elements themselves. Furthermore, with the exception of dyadic transpose, they have the property that columns in the result correspond to columns in the underlying subexpression.[1] In the case of dyadic transpose, columns in the result may correspond to diagonals in the underlying subexpression. Thus, to be precise, we can say that for any given row or column in the result the distance between adjacent elements in the ravel ordering of the underlying subexpressions is a constant.

Because of this property, one can also characterize any particular instance of these functions by a vector, similar to the expansion vector used in the last chapter; that is, the value $A[a_1; \cdots ;a_n]$ will be found at an offset in the underlying subexpression given by

$$offset = \alpha + a_1\gamma_1 + \cdots + a_n\gamma_n$$

for some values of α and γ_i. The task of the code generator is to find the appropriate values for these quantities.

Given this uniform representation, it is perhaps not surprising that structural functions can be composed in a manner not possible with other APL functions; that is, adjacent structural functions can be combined to form a single function, and more efficient code can be generated for the one "super-function" than for the combination of functions separately. An analogy can be made with the composition of transformations in linear algebra. There, each function is represented by a matrix, and function composition corresponds to matrix multiplication. A result produced by two transformations, such as

$$F(G(x))$$

can be more easily computed by first forming the composition

$$(F \circ G)(x)$$

The composition $F \circ G$ is computed by multiplying the two matrices together. The application of this new matrix to x results in the same value as the application of the two functions independently.

1. Note that take and drop may shorten a column, but the essential property of being a column is preserved. There is a problem with overtakes and overdrops, that is takes or drops of lengths greater than the corresponding dimension, which will be discussed shortly.

For the structural functions, the medium for composition is an object called the *stepper*.[2] Each node in the parse tree that represents a structural function has a stepper associated with it. The stepper is characterized by three vectors, each of size n, where n is the rank of the result.

q_i The dimension of the result that the ith dimension of the current node corresponds to.

t_i The index along the ith coordinate of the current node that contributes to the initial element of the result in ravel order; that is, the initial value in the ravel order of the result will be found at location $[t_1;t_2; \cdots ;t_n]$ in the underlying subexpression.

d_i The direction to move along the ith dimension in order to arrive at the next element in the result along the $q_i th$ coordinate. A value $d_i = 1$ indicates a forward (positive) move, whereas a value of –1 indicates a backward (negative) move.

The identity stepper is created by setting q_i to i, t_i to 0, and d_i to 1. A top down traversal of the parse tree is performed to merge adjacent structural functions together into a single stepper. The stepper is initialized at the highest structural function and modified as it is passed through the tree. For example, suppose we are generating code for the expression 1 2 2 ⍉ ¯3 4 5 ↑ ⌽ ⍉ A, where A is an array of rank 3 and shape 6 6 6. Figure 6.1 shows the values of the stepper as they are modified by each node in the parse tree, resulting in the final values as shown at the bottom of the figure. Notice that the rank of the dyadic transpose (2) is smaller than the rank of the arguments to this function (3). For this reason the stepper above the transpose has 2 elements, while the stepper below the transpose function has 3.

---

2. The name *stepper*, as well as much of the technique described in this chapter, is derived from the work of Leo Guibas and Douglas Wyatt, as reported in "Compilation and Delayed Evaluation in APL," Conference record of the 5th ACM Symposium on Principles of Programming Languages, 1978.

functions	q_i	t_i	d_i
identity	0 1	0 0	1 1
1 2 2 ⍉	0 1 1	0 0 0	1 1 1
1 2 2 ⍉ ¯3 4 5 ↑	0 1 1	3 0 0	1 1 1
1 2 2 ⍉ ¯3 4 5 ↑ ⌽	0 1 1	3 0 5	1 1 ¯1
1 2 2 ⍉ ¯3 4 5 ↑ ⌽ ⍉	1 1 0	5 0 3	¯1 1 1

Figure 6.1: Propagation of the Stepper Through a Parse Tree

6.1. Computing the Stepper

The following describes in detail the effect of each of the structural functions on the three vectors that make up the stepper. In each case, n represents the rank of the subexpression, and primed quantities will be used to represent the value of the stepper after the transformation.

6.1.1. Monadic Transpose

Monadic transpose merely reverses each of the three vectors.

$$q'_i \leftarrow q_{n-(i-1)} \quad , 0<i\leq n$$
$$t'_i \leftarrow t_{n-(i-1)} \quad , 0<i\leq n$$
$$d'_i \leftarrow d_{n-(i-1)} \quad , 0<i\leq n$$

6.1.2. Take

Take does not modify the dimensions nor the direction of the result,[3] thus, the values q_i and d_i remain unchanged. The starting

3. According to the APL definition, the elements in the control vector (the left argument) are permitted to be larger in absolute value than the size of the right subexpression for both take and drop. If this is the case the resulting array is suppose to be filled out with 0's. For example, 3 3 ↑ 1 produces a 3 by 3 array with a single 1 in the upper left corner and 0's everywhere else. The code generation scheme described here does not support overtake or overdrop.

location, however, can be modified. Let c_i represent the value of the left (control) argument to the take function, and s_i the size of the subexpression being taken from.

$$\text{if } c_i<0 \text{ then } t'_i \leftarrow t_i+s_i+c_i \quad , 0<i\leq n$$
$$\text{else } t'_i \leftarrow t_i$$

6.1.3. Drop

Like take, drop does not modify the dimensions nor the direction of the result, only the location of the initial value. Let c_i be the value of the left (control) argument to the drop function.

$$\text{if } c_i\geq 0 \text{ then } t'_i \leftarrow t_i+c_i \quad , 0<i\leq n$$
$$\text{else } t'_i \leftarrow t_i$$

6.1.4. Reversal

Assume that we are computing a reversal along the ith coordinate. The only values to be changed will be t_i (since the initial location will move from one end of the row to the other) and d_i (since the direction of movement along the ith dimension is reversed). Let s_i represent the size of the right argument.

$$t'_i \leftarrow s_i - t_i - 1$$
$$d'_i \leftarrow -d_i$$

6.1.5. Dyadic Transpose

Dyadic transpose is complicated by the fact that the result rank and shape may be smaller than the subexpression rank and shape. Let c_i represent the value of the left (control) argument to the function.

$$q'_i \leftarrow q_j \quad , j = c_i - 1 \quad , 0<i\leq n$$
$$t'_i \leftarrow t_j \quad , j = c_i - 1 \quad , 0<i\leq n$$
$$d'_i \leftarrow d_j \quad , j = c_i - 1 \quad , 0<i\leq n$$

Notice that the resulting stepper may be larger than the original stepper. This occurs in Figure 6.1, for example.

Thus, the APL compiler does not support this feature and will produce incorrect results (according to the definition) in these cases.

6.2. The Accessor

Having propagated the stepper values through a sequence of adjacent structural functions, we can use the resulting information to determine how to generate code for the operation. If we let A represent the underlying subexpression (the expression immediately below the structural functions), then clearly the initial value in the ravel ordering of the result is given by:

$$\mathrm{A}\,[\,t_1;\,\cdots\,;t_n\,]$$

If we let e_i represent the expansion vector for A, we know from (5.2) that this value is found at an offset given by

$$\alpha = t_1 e_1 + \cdots + t_n e_n$$

The vector q_i tells us how the dimensions of the result are being transposed. The vector d_i tells us in which direction to move along each dimension in order to return the next element. We can combine these with e_i to form a new vector, which will act very much like the expansion vector. Consider the values defined by the following formula:

$$\gamma_i \leftarrow \sum_{q_j=i} d_j e_j$$

The offset of result element $a_1;\cdots;a_n$ can be given in terms of these quantities as follows:

$$offset = \alpha + (a_1\gamma_1 + \cdots + a_n\gamma_n)$$

Given this equation, it is now easy to generate code for the structural functions. As in the last chapter, let $offset$ represent the position of the desired value in the ravel order of the result. The goal is to compute $offset'$, a position in the underlying subexpression where the desired value will be found. Let s_i represent the size of the result. By repeatedly dividing by s_i we obtain the ith position in the vector form of the requested offset.

```
offset' = α
for i = n to 1 by −1 do begin
    offset' = offset' + (offset mod s_i) × γ_i
    offset = offset div s_i
    end
{ compute value of subexpression at offset' }
```

6.3. Sequential Access

As we saw in the last chapter, if it can be determined at compile time that a result will be accessed in sequential ravel order, it is often possible for the compiler to take advantage of this information to produce better code. So it is with the structural functions. To see how this can be accomplished, consider the sequence of requests passed to an expression of size 2 by 3 by 3. Figure 6.2 shows the sequence of requests, along with the vector representing the subscripts of the position being requested. Notice how these values increase in an odometer like fashion.

position	subscript	computation
		$offset' = \alpha$
0	0 0 0	
		$offset' = offset' + \gamma_1$
1	0 0 1	
		$offset' = offset' + \gamma_1$
2	0 0 2	
		$offset' = offset' + \gamma_1 + \gamma_2 - 3\times\gamma_1$
3	0 1 0	
		$offset' = offset' + \gamma_1$
4	0 1 1	
. . .		
8	0 2 2	
		$offset' = offset' + \gamma_1 + \gamma_2 - 3\times\gamma_1 + \gamma_3 - 3\times\gamma_2$
9	1 0 0	

Figure 6.2: Computation of Elements in Sequential Order

The figure also shows how the computation of the next offset for the subexpression can be computed easily in terms of prior values. The index $offset'$ is initialized to α in the shape phase. Thereafter, *after* every computation the value of the index is updated. To update the index, we add the value γ_n to it; however, if the rightmost value in the odometer has turned over, we want to subtract off a number of values equal to γ_n times s_n, the size of the last dimension, before adding γ_{n-1}.

We can precompute the computation performed when an odometer position turns over by introducing a new vector:

$$\delta_i = \gamma_i - \gamma_{i+1} \times s_{i+1} \quad , i < n$$
$$\delta_n = \gamma_n$$

The value δ represents the amount needed to correctly reach the next position, at the same time correcting the previous dimension that has "stepped off" the end of the row. Using these values, the code for structural functions in the sequential case can be given as follows:

Shape Phase

$offset' = \alpha$

Value Phase

```
{ compute value of subexpression at offset' }
t = s_n
for i = n to 1 by -1 do begin
    offset' = offset' + δ_i
    if (offset+1) mod t = 0 then
        t = t×s_{i-1}
    else
        break
    end
```

Note that t is a temporary variable, not to be confused with the array t_i that forms part of the stepper. Note also that the computation of the result of the subexpression takes place before $offset'$ is updated, instead of after the computation of $offset'$, as in the general case. The computation of the revised value requires at most $2n$ multiplications and divisions, but often less. This contrasts with the code for the general case, which always requires n multiplications and $2n$ divisions to compute the index for each value.

6.4. A Nonobvious Optimization

We recall that the following code was proposed to compute the value of $offset'$ in the general case:

```
offset' = α
for i = n to 1 by −1 do begin
        offset' = offset' + (offset mod s_i) × γ_i
        offset = offset div s_i
        end
{ compute value of subexpression at offset' }
```

As we have already noted, this code requires n multiplications and $2n$ divisions to compute each value of *offset'*. Using the values δ_i given in the last section, we can reduce this cost by one-third. In contrast to previous discussions, we will here first present the generated code and then argue why it is correct.

The optimized code for the general case of structural functions is as follows:

```
offset' = α
for i = n to 1 by −1 do begin
        offset' = offset' + offset × δ_i
        offset = offset div s_i
        end
{ compute value of subexpression at offset' }
```

Let $\kappa_i = offset$ **div** e_i, where e_i represents the expansion vector for the result being computed. Observe that $\kappa_{i-1} = \kappa_i$ **div** s_i and $k_n = offset$. It is not difficult to see that the value placed into *offset'* by the loop represents

$$\alpha + \sum_{i=1}^{n} \kappa_i \, \delta_i$$

Expanding this, by using the definition of δ, we get

$$\alpha + \left(\sum_{i=1}^{n-1} \kappa_i \gamma_i - \kappa_i \, \gamma_{i+1} \, s_{i+1} \right) + \kappa_n \gamma_n$$

Factoring out the common values of γ_i, this gives us

$$\alpha + \kappa_1 \gamma_1 + \sum_{i=2}^{n} (\kappa_i - \kappa_{i-1} \, s_i) \, \gamma_i$$

Following our observation on κ_{i-1}

$$\alpha + \kappa_1 \gamma_1 + \sum_{i=2}^{n} (\kappa_i - (\kappa_i \textbf{ div } s_i) \, s_i) \, \gamma_i$$

The quantity being summed over can be simplified to

$$\alpha + \kappa_1\gamma_1 + \sum_{i=2}^{n}(\kappa_i \ \mathbf{mod}\ s_i)\ \gamma_i$$

We replace the κ_i terms by their definition, so as to express the result in terms of *offset*:

$$\alpha + (offset\ \mathbf{div}\ e_1)\ \gamma_1 + \sum_{i=2}^{n}((offset\ \mathbf{div}\ e_i)\ \mathbf{mod}\ s_i)\ \gamma_i$$

From (5.7), however, we know that $offset$ **div** e_1 is equal to a_1, and $(offset$ **div** $e_i)$ **mod** s_i is equal to a_i. Thus, the result is observed to be

$$\alpha + \sum_{i=1}^{n} a_i\ \gamma_i$$

which is indeed the desired element. The improved code produces the same results as the original but requires only n divisions per element, in place of the $2n$ required by the original.

Chapter 7

Space Inefficient Functions

Not all APL functions can be adapted easily to the demand driven space efficient implementation technique described in the last few chapters. In this chapter we consider the remaining APL functions and show how, despite this fact, code can be generated for them that combines smoothly with the code generated for other functions.

The functions that remain can be divided into two groups. A binary function is *semi-space efficient* if it is space efficient with respect to only one of its two arguments. In truth, some of the structural functions described in the last chapter, as well as the function reshape, were only semi-space efficient. This is because the left (control) argument had to be gathered in its entirety during the shape phase, before any values could be produced. In these cases, however, the left argument was typically a scalar or small vector and could therefore be considered to be part of the function. There are two remaining semi-space efficient functions for which this is not the case, namely, index (dyadic iota) and membership (dyadic epsilon).

We call all other remaining functions *collectors*, since they collect all their values in one place before passing any of them onto other functions. These collector functions are the following:

box (input quad)
rank and shape
deal and roll
sort (grade up and grade down)
user function calls

Lastly, in this chapter we discuss the code produced for the branching arrow.

7.1. Semi-Space Efficient Functions

The operation of the two functions index (dyadic iota) and membership (dyadic epsilon) are very similar but in some ways just the opposite of each other. The first results in an object the same size and shape as its right argument; the second, the same as its left. They both determine whether an element of one of the arguments occurs in the second, one returning a position and the other a yes/no answer.

Despite the earlier claim, one could, in fact, use a space efficient implementation technique for these functions. Take membership, for example. The following algorithm could be used to produce a single value for the membership function:

Value Phase

```
{ code to compute left argument at position offset }
result = 0
for offset' = 1 to (size of right argument) do begin
    { code to compute right argument at position offset' }
    if (left value = right value) then begin
        result = 1
        break
        end
    end
```

The disadvantage of this code, clearly, is that in the worst case it must search the entire right side for each value that it produces. If the left side contains n elements, and the right side contains m elements, this can take time proportional to their product, $O(nm)$. If one is willing to sacrifice a bit of memory for a considerable savings in speed, we can sort all the elements of the right argument once during the shape phase, at a cost proportional to $m \log m$. Having sorted the right side, a binary search (cost $O(\log m)$) can be used to determine whether each element of the left occurs in the right side. Since there are n elements from the left side, the resulting cost is $O((n+m) \log m)$. In one example that tested the effectiveness of this technique, a 500 element vector being compared to itself used 334.2 milliseconds with the original method and 140.6 milliseconds with the alternative algorithm.

The generated code for membership (dyadic epsilon) is therefore as follows:

Shape Phase

gather the right argument into a vector and sort it

Value Phase

compute the value of the left argument at position *offset*
perform a binary search on the sorted right argument to
see if the element appears, returning 1 or 0 (true or false).

The code for index (dyadic iota) is similar

Shape Phase

sort the left argument (which must be a vector)

Value Phase

compute the value of the right argument at position *offset*
perform a binary search of the sorted left argument to see if
the element appears, returning the value of the grade-up
vector at the position in the sorted left argument (this is
the index of the position in the original subexpression),
or the size of the left argument plus one if it does not appear.

7.2. Collectors

For the few remaining functions, the basic implementation strategy is as follows. During the shape phase the arguments (if any) are collected and stored in a temporary location. The functions are then performed on the temporary values, and the results again are placed into other temporaries. During the value phase elements are read out of these locations, just as they are from leaf nodes, such as identifiers.

7.3. Branching

Before we can describe the code generated for the branching function, it is first necessary to step back and describe in more general terms the structure of the code generated for an APL function.

Within each C program generated for an APL function there is declared a local integer variable, *stmtno*, which contains the number of the statement currently being executed. As long as this value remains in the range of valid statements, execution continues. This is accomplished by structuring the code in the following way:

```
stmtno = 1;
while (stmtno)
    switch (stmtno) {
        default:
            stmtno = 0;
            break;
        case 1:
            stmtno = 1;
            { code for the first statement }

        case 2:
            stmtno = 2;
            { code for the second statement }
         . . .

        case n:
            stmtno = n;
            { code for the nth statement }
            stmtno = 0;
        }
```

By initializing the value of stmtno to 1, the first statement will be the first one executed. Since no *break* statement appears following the code for the first APL statement, control will flow into the second statement, and so on, unless explicitly redirected. Following the last statement, the variable stmtno will be set to zero, causing the loop to terminate.

Thus, to explicitly branch to a new statement it is only necessary to modify the value of the variable stmtno and execute a C *break* to get out of the switch statement. If the value of stmtno is nonzero, the loop will continue and the case corresponding to the new statement will be selected. If the value of the branch is out of range, the default case will be selected and the variable stmtno will be set to 0. Thus, the code generated for a branch statement can be described as follows:

```
{ code to compute the size of the label expression }
if size of label expression > 0 then begin
    { compute first value in label expression }
    stmtno = result;
    break
    end
```

Notice that if the label expression contains no values execution continues with the next statement.

Chapter 8

Compiling for a Vector Machine

Machines that can execute several arithmetic operations in parallel have existed for many years. Nevertheless, the software needed to make effective use of this ability has been slow in developing. Most current high-level languages, of the Algol-Fortran-Pascal variety, are not designed for the expression of parallelism. Thus, the attempt to use parallelism has taken two general approaches. The first approach is to analyze source code statically in an attempt to recognize operations (such as loops) that could potentially be executed in parallel. As might be expected, this task is very difficult and has met with only limited success. A second approach is to develop new programming languages with explicit parallel instructions. The acceptance of new languages is slow, however, and this has the drawback of producing yet another programming language that is available on only a limited number of machines in a limited number of locations.

The language APL is unique in that it has enjoyed relatively widespread use for a number of years, has existing implementations on a number of machines, and most importantly is a language in which the recognition of potential parallelism is relatively easy.

This chapter will describe how the algorithms developed in the previous chapters could be modified to make use of vector instructions.

8.1. Machine Model

The algorithms that we present will make use of instructions for a hypothetical vector machine. This abstract machine is similar to existing vector machines, such as the CRAY, the CDC STAR-100, or the IBM 3090. In addition to the usual repertoire of scalar instructions, we assume the existence of vector-vector instructions (such as adding two vectors together to produce a third vector) and vector-scalar instructions (such as adding a scalar to each element of a vector). Each vector operation takes an argument that indicates the size of the vector being acted upon.

In addition to arithmetic vector commands, we will also make use of one additional command. This command takes a vector of addresses (which need not be contiguous) and produces a vector of values from the corresponding positions in memory. The CRAY-1 has a simplified form of this command, where the addresses must be in an arithmetic progression. As we shall see, such progressions are oftentimes (although not always) generated by the APL compiler. In any case, we shall assume the more general capability.

8.2. Columns and Request Forms

We define a *column* to be a vector formed by fixing all but one dimension in an array; in APL notation a column is described as $A[r_1;r_2;...;r_{k-1};;r_{k+1};...;r_n]$ for some fixed constants r_1 through r_n. There are three important quantities that characterize a column. The column *axis* (which we will denote α) is the position of the free axis. The column *start* (denoted β) is the offset position of the element $A[r_1;r_2;...;r_{k-1};0;r_{k+1};...;r_n]$ in the ravel sequence of A. Finally the column *step* (denoted δ) is the distance (in ravel sequence) from one element in a column to the next. In terms of the expansion vector, δ is equal to e_α. Thus the ravel position of the element with index i in a column is $\beta + \mathrm{i} \times \delta$.

A subexpression can be given a request for values in one of three forms. An *Arithmetic Progression Vector* (APV) is characterized by five quantities. Besides the column axis, start and step (α, β and δ), there is a vector offset, denoted by a value σ

between 0 and $(\rho A)[\alpha] - 1$, and a vector length (ω). The values being requested are column positions σ through $\sigma + \omega - 1$. Since five scalar quantities are used to request a large number of values, the APV is a very efficient encoding of a request and will always be preferred to other forms. An APV can only be used, however, for elements contiguous along some dimension in the matrix representation, so other request forms are sometimes necessary.

A *column vector* (CV) consists of a column description (α, β and δ), a vector (ν) of column offsets (values between zero and the length of the column), and a vector length (ω). The statement $\nu \leftarrow \sigma + (\iota\ \omega)$ can be used to convert an arithmetic progression vector to a column vector.

An *offset vector* (OV) is a vector (θ) of offset positions into the substructure being constructed (ravel order assumed). The statement $\theta \leftarrow \beta + \delta \times \nu$ converts a column vector into an offset vector.

The particular form used to request values from a subexpression is determined at compile time. In subsequent discussions in this chapter we will describe how the request form is altered by various APL functions. A few operations (assignment in particular) generate loops to gather values. These loops always generate an APV, it being the most efficient encoding for a request for values. For example, assuming we are generating code for an expression A, an assignment produces the following code.

Shape Phase

```
α = ρρ A               /* rank of A */
δ = 1                  /* distance between adjacent elements */
ω = ¯1 ↑ ρ A           /* distance to next column */
limit = × / ρ A        /* size of A */
σ = 0;
```

Value Phase

```
for β = 0 to limit − 1 by ω do begin
    { code to compute results described by APV }
    A[β + δ × ι ω] ← value
    end
```

Not all the APL functions are easily vectorizable. Functions such as sort and membership, for example, are more easily performed using scalar operations. In expressions involving both vectorized and scalar functions, code must be produced to convert a vector request (an APV or an offset vector) into an index. In this case a temporary vector of length ω is allocated during the shape phase. Each iteration of the vector request requires a loop to fill the values of the temporary one by one. The following illustrates the code generated assuming the vector request is given by an APV, the code for the other two request forms being similar.

$offset' = \beta + \sigma \times \delta$
for i = 0 **to** ω **do begin**
  { compute scalar value at location $offset'$ }
  temp[i] = value
  $offset' = offset' + \delta$
  end

At the other end of the parse tree, our machine model assumes that simple instructions can be generated to fill an entire vector with values from a leaf node, such as an identifier or a constant. The only small complication here involves identifiers which may possibly be, but are not certainly, scalar. In this case, code must be generated to check the rank dynamically, and if the identifier is scalar, return a vector where each position contains the same scalar value.

8.3. Code Generation

As we have already noted, not all APL functions are amenable to vectorization. In the following sections we will describe the algorithms for those functions that can be so handled; all other functions will generate the same code as described in the previous chapters.

8.3.1. Reduction

For reduction we can use the vector instructions to compute an entire column of the result in one loop. If the request is given by an offset vector, we can use a vector form of equation 5.7 to compute a sequence of new offsets (note that the difference between adjacent elements being reduced will all be given by the value of the expansion vector along the axis of the reduction, that is e_i). The generated code is then identical to that given in Chapter 5, with the exception that vector instructions are used to modify the values $offset'$.

If the request for values is given by an arithmetic progression vector or a column vector, it would be beneficial to try to preserve the form. This can be done, if we note that the only values that need be modified to change the request given to the reduction function into the request given to the child function are the scalar quantities β and δ. The modification for the latter depends upon whether the axis of reduction (call it i) is greater or smaller than the axis of the request (α).

Shape Phase

> **if** $\alpha <$ i **then**
> $\quad\delta' = \delta \times s_i$
> **else**
> $\quad\delta' = \delta$

Value Phase

> *result = vector identity for operation*
> $\beta' = (\beta$ **div** $e_i)(e_i s_i) + (s_i - 1)e_i + (\beta$ **mod** $e_i)$
> **for** counter $= 1$ **to** s_i **do begin**
> $\quad$ { compute value of child at requested positions }
> $\quad$ *result = value op result*
> $\quad\beta' = \beta' - e_i$
> $\quad$ **end**

The various optimizations described in Chapter 5 for the scalar case, such as moving the computation of $(s_i - 1)e_i$ to the shape phase, are also applicable to this code and will not be repeated here.

8.3.2. Scan

It is useful to generate vector code for scan only if it can be determined at compile time that the axis of the request (α) is different from the axis of the scan and if the request form is an APV or column vector. It is only under these conditions that the loop for the scan will execute the same number of times for each element of the result. As was the case with the code generated for reduction, the algorithms that in Chapter 5 modified *offset* are here simply changed to modify β. Unlike the case for reduction, for scan the value δ used by the child is the same as that given to the scan function.

Value Phase

$result$ = identity for operation
$a_i = (\beta$ **div** $e_i)$ **mod** s_i
$\beta' = offset$
for counter = 1 **to** a_i **do begin**
{ compute the vector value of the subexpression at β' }
$result = value\ op\ result$
$\beta' = \beta' - e_i$
end

8.3.3. Compression and Expansion

As is the case with the scan function, vector forms are useful for compression and expansion only if it can be determined at compile time that the axis of the function is orthogonal to the axis of the request[1]. If this is the case, then all elements of the requested column can be computed together.

The shape phase code for the functions compression and expansion is the same as in the scalar case. For requests given by an APV or column vector, the code is identical to the scalar case, with β taking the place of $offset$. For example, the code for compression is as follows:

Value Phase

$a_i = (\beta$ **div** $e_i)$ **mod** s_i
$a' = \mathrm{v}[a_i]$
$\beta' = ((\beta$ **div** $(e_i s_i))s'_i) + a')e_i + (\beta$ **mod** $e_i)$
{ compute the value at β' in the left argument }

For requests given by an offset vector, the entire vector is modified, with θ taking the place of β in the above.

1. This is not strictly true. The orthogonality of the function axis and the request axis insures that all elements of the resulting column will be computed in the same fashion. The case in which the axes coincide could be handled if we were willing to add some further instructions to our machine model. Unfortunately, the code sequences for these two cases are so different that if it could not be determined at compile time which case to use, *both* sequences would have to be generated.

8.3.4. Catenation

In describing the code generated for the catenation function, we will again assume that at compile time it can be determined that the axis of catenation is orthogonal to the axis of the request[2] and that the request is by APV or column vector. Given these conditions, all elements of the requested column will lie in either one of the subexpressions or the other. Testing β suffices to determine in which half they occur, and modifications to β will produce the new requests.

Value Phase

$a_i = (\beta$ **div** $e_i)$ **mod** (s_L+s_R)
if $a_i < s_L$ **then begin**
    $\beta'_L = (\beta$ **div** $(e_i(s_L+s_R)))\times s_L)+a_i)\times e_i+(\beta$ **mod** $e_i)$
    { compute value of left subexpression at β'_L }
    end
else begin
    $a_i = a_i - s_L$
    $\beta'_R = (\beta$ **div** $(e_i(s_L+s_R)))\times s_R)+a_i)\times e_i+(\beta$ **mod** $e_i)$
    { compute value of right subexpression at β'_R }
    end

8.3.5. Dyadic Rotation

The code for the vector form of dyadic rotation divides into two cases. If it can be determined at compile time that the axis of request is equal to the axis of the function, and if the request is by APV or column vector, then all elements of the requested column will be rotated by a fixed amount that can be determined by replacing *offset* by β in equation 5.9. The request is changed into a column vector, and each element of the vector is modified by the amount.

In all other cases the request is first changed into an offset vector. The vector θ then replaces *offset* in 5.9, resulting in a vector of differences. This vector is used to modify the original offset vector, forming the new addresses.

---

2. Similar comments hold for this case as for the case of compression and expansion; namely, we could handle the coincidental case if we were willing to add further instructions to our machine model.

8.3.6. Structural Functions

As we noted at the beginning of Chapter 6, the characterization of the structural functions is the fact that they carry columns into columns; thus, they should ideally be suited for vectorization. If a request is by APV or offset vector, it suffices to determine how the base is changed and to determine the new distance between adjacent elements. These are given by the functions q^{-1} (the inverse of the q_i of chapter 6) and γ_i.

Shape Phase

$$\alpha' = q^{-1}[\alpha]$$
$$\delta' = \gamma_{\alpha'}$$

The code to compute the value of β to pass to the child is the same as the code to compute $offset'$ in the scalar case.

Value Phase

$\beta' = \alpha$
for i $= n$ **to** 1 **by** -1 **do begin**
 $\beta' = \beta' + (\beta$ **mod** $s_i) \times \gamma_i$
 $\beta = \beta$ **div** s_i
{ compute vector value of subexpression at β' }

The optimizations described in chapter 6 can also be applied in this situation. In the case in which the request is by offset vector, the vector θ replaces the scalar β in the above.

8.3.7. Outer Product and Subscript

If the request to an outer product is given by an APV or column vector, then the result will always be generated by a vector from one argument and by a scalar from the other argument, depending upon whether α is greater or less than the rank of the right argument. Let t represent the number of elements in the right argument.

$\beta' = \beta$ **div** t
{ produce value (result1) of left argument at β' }
$\beta'' = \beta$ **mod** t
{ produce value (result2) of right argument at β'' }
res = result1 op result2

If the request is by offset vector, two new offset vectors are generated.

$\theta' = \theta$ **div** t
{ produce value (result1) of left argument at β' }
$\theta'' = \theta$ **mod** t
{ produce value (result2) of right argument at β'' }
res = result1 op result2

Subscripting in APL is in many ways quite different from subscripting in other languages. As we noted in Chapter 4, the semicolon function used in subscripting is very similar to an outer product. Consider a vector of requests for elements from the expression A[B;C]. This request is first divided into separate request vectors for B and for C, as is done for outer products. (In the situation in which more than one semicolon is present, they can be treated as multiple occurrences of binary functions.) These result in offset vectors of equal size. These vectors are then combined to produce an offset vector into the subscripted expression (A in this example). The result of this subexpression in response to the request is then returned as the result of the entire subscripted expression.

Chapter 9

Epilogue

The APL compiler project can be said to have achieved its major goal: successfully showing how optimized space efficient algorithms can be generated by a compiler for a language with indeterminate data objects using demand driven evaluation techniques. Nevertheless, this is only a small part of any production quality programming system. The larger issues of integrating the methods presented here into the more familiar APL workspace environment have not been addressed.

An interesting observation concerns the amount of functionality exhibited by a single APL statement versus a single statement in, say, Pascal. The more operations there are in an expression, the greater is the likelihood that the demand driven space efficient techniques described in Chapters 3 through 7 can be applied to reduce the amount of intermediate storage necessary to produce a result. Thus, the infamous "one-liner," considered almost an art form among supporters of APL (Perlis 1979), and strongly denounced by detractors of the language (Dijkstra 1972), is shown to have a practical benefit. Of course, one could distinguish between "physical" one-liners (programs written on one line) and "conceptual" one-liners (programs written without looping structure). In the latter case, simple dataflow techniques, which are extensions of the methods described in Chapter 2, could be used to determine statements that could be combined to facilitate optimized execution.

On the negative side, as we noted in Chapter 1, it is difficult for a true compiler (a compiler that executes as a separate process from the running program and that may not even be present at execution time) to provide the same type of interactive design and debugging tools as an interpreter. Ideally, one would like to integrate the compiler and an interpreter, thus providing the advantages of both in a complete development environment along the Lisp model.

If there is any glaring omission in the material presented in this book, it is the lack of any detailed timings or comparisons to code generated using other techniques. While I admit that such statistics can be useful, they can also be deceptive and difficult, not only to obtain but to understand as well. The APL compiler was developed on a badly overloaded DEC VAX 750 computer. It is, however, written in C and is designed to run on any UNIX system, which represents a wide spectrum of machines. In reporting absolute timings of the generated code, such as those given at the end of Chapter 2, should I report the figures given by the *time* command on my overloaded 750? This was the technique used near the end of Chapter 2, where the intent was to compare execution times of various programs all produced by the APL compiler. Alternatively, should I have tried to obtain permission to use a faster UNIX processor and hence obtain more impressive, but presumably not any more truthful, statistics? Perhaps neither figure should be taken at face value but should be divided by some normalization factor, such as the mythical MIPS number. Even so doing this would only provide a rough characterization of our system; to be useful we would need a comparison to other systems. However, there are few other APL compilers and none (to my knowledge) running on UNIX machines; and how do we integrate in the operating system dependent factors into the timings?

Recently, an entire book has been devoted to the technique of timing Lisp systems and a comparison of various Lisp implementations (Gabriel 1986). One can hope that eventually such a study can be performed for APL systems, but until that point the whole question of timings, both absolute and relative, is fraught with danger. It is for this reason that I have ignored the question of timings altogether and have chosen to stick to a safer path by being concerned only with algorithms. Despite this fact, it is my hope that some readers will have found the techniques presented in this book interesting as algorithms for their own sake and that this book may, in some small way, influence future implementations of this wonderfully complex language.

Appendix 1

The Language of the APL Compiler

As we noted in Chapter 1, in pursuing this project we were interested in developing a compiler for an APL-*like* language, not necessarily in constructing a system for textbook APL. Thus, we did not feel constrained by any requirements to conform exactly to any existing standard for the language. In this appendix we describe the major deviations in our system from standard APL.

Except as noted elsewhere in this appendix, the APL statement syntax has been left unchanged. Detailed descriptions of this syntax can be found in many textbooks, such as (Gilman 1976) or (Polivka 1975).

Omissions

A number of standard APL functions are not implemented in the APL compiler.

The following functions were not implemented because the algorithms needed to accommodate them were deemed similar to algorithms used in more common functions, and thus little additional experience or knowledge would be gained by including them:

encode
format
lamination

The following functions were not implemented because they did not easily fit into our demand driven execution technique and required a large run-time support system.

execute
matrix inverse and least squares
quote-quad for general expressions
files
system functions and variables
latent expression
tracing

Workspaces

The concept of the APL workspace is not supported. Workspace commands are not recognized and result in syntax errors if used. Built-in functions, such as []WA or []LC, that refer to workspace parameters are not recognized.

Scoping Rules

The APL dynamic scoping rule has been replaced by a simple two-level static scoping. Variables are either local to the program in which they are declared or global to all procedures. Variables declared outside of any program are automatically given the attribute global (see below).

System variables, such as []IO and []PP, are true global variables and are not automatically restored to their previous values on procedure exit.

Order of Execution

The order of execution is not guaranteed to be strictly right to left. Certain functions, such as reshape or compress, may evaluate their left argument before their right argument. Thus, expressions that depend upon a side effect may produce unpredictable results. An example is using a variable while at the same time redefining the variable elsewhere in the expression. The following statements are almost certain to produce a result other than the one intended.

$$X \leftarrow 3\ 3\ \rho\ \iota\ 9$$
$$(X \leftarrow \iota\ 5\ ) + X$$

This is not a violation of the standard, but is rather what the standard calls a "consistent extension".

Commutative Functions

Many APL programmers mistakenly believe that APL requires that all expressions be evaluated strictly right to left. This is true even in such situations as a reduction, for example,

$$+/\ \iota\ 6$$

where, because a commutative function is being used, the order of evaluation presumably does not matter. In fact, the APL standard permits any order, once more under the name of "consistent extensions". In these cases we have felt free to sometimes change the order of evaluation to left to right, thereby permitting other optimizations that may depend upon the order in which expressions are accessed.

Demand Driven Semantics

The APL compiler uses a demand driven, or lazy evaluation semantics. The difference between this and conventional APL semantics is most easily seen in expressions that would produce an error under the conventional interpretation but would not under the modified semantics. An example is

$$0\ 1\ /\ 2\ 3 \div 0\ 4$$

A conventional interpreter would produce a run-time error, since 2 cannot be divided by 0. The demand driven technique would only attempt the divide instruction for values that were needed in other parts of the computation. Since the first element of the vector produced by the division is eliminated by the compression function, it can never be used. Thus, no attempt would be made to divide 2 by 0, and no error would be reported. Again, the APL standard permits this as a consistent extension.

Heading and Declarations

The format for procedure headings has been altered considerably. Local variables are no longer declared on the same line as the procedure heading. Instead, a procedure heading can be followed by any number of declaration statements.

The format for a heading is the symbol ∇, followed by an optional assignment part, followed by an optional left argument name, followed by the function name, followed by the right argument name. Niladic functions are not supported (see below).

The syntax for a declaration is an attribute followed by a list of variable names. Attributes are divided into classes (**global**, **function**) and types (**var**, **int**, **bit**, **char**, **real**). An attribute consists of a class and/or a type. Thus, the following are legal declarations and have the indicated meanings:

var a, b, c	local variables, type unknown
global int i, j	global integer variables
char global x	global character variable
fun p	function p, type unknown

All global variables and functions used in a procedure that have not been previously encountered must be declared; that is, functions and globals must be declared prior to their first encounter. Local variables need not be declared if their first occurrence is as the left argument in an assignment, but from a stylistic point of view some argue that it is better to declare all variables. Variables and functions need not have declared types; however, specifying types allows the compiler to produce better code.

System variables, such as []IO and []PP, cannot be declared local to a procedure.

Niladic Functions

A major problem with compilers is that they must, of necessity, determine the type of each token in an expression long before the expression is ever executed. It is for this reason that the APL compiler requires users to declare in the heading of a function both global names and functions that have not been previously seen. There is one (admittedly uncommon) situation in which even this amount of information is not sufficient to completely determine the meaning of all tokens. Consider the following fragment from a function:

FUN F, G

. . .

X ← F G *expression*

There are two possible interpretations:

1. F is a niladic function, G is a dyadic function, or
2. Both F and G are monadic functions.

Without further information the compiler cannot determine which of these two cases is correct. For the APL compiler we took the expedient solution of disallowing niladic functions. Some have argued that this is too radical a solution and that a better alternative would have been to introduce optional declarations for the valence of functions, as well as for their result rank and type. The compiler then could issue error messages in those few cases in which it could not be determined from context what the correct interpretation should be, and the user could insert informative declarations.

As with the change from dynamic to static scoping, the decision to eliminate niladic functions was merely a convenience and is not intrinsic to the space efficient demand driven method of execution outlined in this book.

Overtake

Standard APL uses the take function (↑) both to extract a subportion of a larger array and to extend an array with fill values; that is, the expression 2 2 ↑ 3 3 ρ ι 9 returns the array

```
1 2
4 5
```

but 4 4 ↑ 3 3 ρ ι 9 yields

```
1 2 3 0
4 5 6 0
7 8 9 0
0 0 0 0
```

The Guibas and Wyatt algorithm which we use in generating code for Take, as described in Chapter 6, does not correctly handle overtake, so we do not support this feature.

Data Types and Storage

If a variable is given a specific data type, either by declaration or inference from the program text, it retains that type throughout execution. A simple program illustrates how this differs from most APL systems. Consider the program

```
X ← 2
L: X ← 2 × X
→ L
```

On conventional APL systems X would at some point cease being represented internally as an integer and would become a floating point value. With the APL compiler X would always remain an integer but would at some point overflow. No code is generated to detect this overflow; however, on some machines this would cause a program interrupt.

Although the datatype boolean is treated as distinct from integer by the declaration statements and by the type inference algorithms, for the purposes of storage we treat them as the same. While this is inefficient in terms of storage, it simplified our generated code for assignment and identifiers. There is, however, nothing inherent in the algorithms that we have described that requires us to waste storage for boolean datatypes in this manner, and with slightly more care in the generation of code for these two situations a true binary datatype could be achieved without any change to the other code generation algorithms.

Exceptional or Special Cases

In designing the algorithms to be used by each of the various APL functions, we concentrated on efficiently implementing the most common or general cases. Our code will often fail (hopefully issuing an error message first) if conditions for these cases are not satisfied, even in situations in which other APL systems would continue. In some cases the correct answer fortuitously results from the code for the general case, and we suspect that this is why many exceptional cases were permitted by earlier APL systems. At other times, we are not so fortunate.

For example, we require that the argument to iota be an integer scalar. Many APL systems also permit the argument to be a vector of size 1, although interestingly not usually an array of size 1 in each dimension.

Functions that have special cases that we do not support include catenation and inner product.

The program MAIN

Statements, including declarations, that are outside the range of any procedure body are assumed to refer to the main program. These statements can be intermixed with procedure declarations, however, from a stylistic point of view this should be avoided. All variables in the main program are given the attribute **global**.

Labelled statements are not permitted in the main program, due to the difficulty in differentiating them from functions being defined in direct definition form (Iverson 1980).

System Variables

The following system variables can be referenced but not assigned.

[]TS Returns an integer vector containing the current year, month, day, hour, minute, and second.

[]AV Returns an 256 element character vector representing the ASCII character sequence.

The following system variables can be both assigned to and referenced.

[]IO Sets the index origin for indexing. Returns the current index origin.

[]PP Sets the number of positions used in printing integer and real variables. Returns the current printing precision.

[]PW Sets the number of characters to be used in printing integer and real variables. Returns the current printing width.

[]RL Sets a seed value for the random number generator used in roll and deal. Returns the current random number.

Format of Output

The number of characters to be used in printing any element is completely determined by the system variables printing precision and printing width (above), instead of by the data being printed.

Appendix 2

A Simple Example

This appendix will analyze the code generated for an expression when the compiler has almost perfect information; that is, it knows the type, rank, and shape of all functions. The expression we will consider is a variation on the classic primes idiom given in Chapter 2, only instead of returning the list of primes, we will merely count their number. The expression can thus be given as

$$A \leftarrow +/\ (2 = +\!\!\not/0 = (\iota\ 200)\ \circ.|\ \ \iota\ 200)$$

We will consider each function in this expression individually, and we will show how each contributes to the generated code. First, however, we will present the code in its entirety:

```
i9 = 200;
i13 = 200;
i12 = 200;
i15 = (i13 - 1) * i12;
i20 = 200;
settrs(&trs1, INT, 0, &i_main[1]);
i1 = talloc(&trs1);
mp1.ip = trs1.value.ip;
res15.i = 0;
for (i3 = 0; i3 < i20; i3++) {
      res11.i = 0;
      i4 = i15 + i3;
      for (i14 = i13 - 1; i14 >= 0; i14--) {
            i6 = i4 - i9 * (i5 = i4 / i9);
            res11.i += (0 == ((i6 + 1) % (i5 + 1)));
            i4 -= i12;
      }
      res15.i += (2 == res11.i);
}
(*mp1.ip = res15.i);
assign(&a, &trs1);
```

We now analyze each function in this example in turn.

Assignment

The code generated for assignment consists of the following pieces:

Shape Phase

```
settrs(&trs1, INT, 0, &i_main[1]);
i1 = talloc(&trs1);
mp1.ip = trs1.value.ip;
```

Value Phase

```
(*mp1.ip = res15.i);
```

Finish Phase

```
assign(&a, &trs1);
```

The identifier *trs1* represents a type, rank, shape, and value structure; an object that can contain all the information about an identifier. The procedure *settrs* is used to copy values into the first three fields of such a structure. Since the size of the result is known at compile time, all the parameters in the call on *settrs* are constants. Had the sizes not been known, code would have been generated prior to the call on *settrs* that would have placed the type, rank, and shape information into variables, and these would be passed to the function.

The expression &i_main[1] represents a pointer to a location in the integer (hence, the i_ prefix) constant pool for this function. Since the result is a scalar, the shape is presumably of little importance, nevertheless, a one (1) value is stored at this location.

The function *talloc* allocates a block of memory, placing the address into the value field of the trs structure passed as argument. (A minor point, the & in front of trs1 in both this and the call on *settrs* is necessary because of the call-by-value semantics of C. Since in both cases trs1 is modified, it is necessary to pass a pointer to the structure, rather than the value of the structure.) The *value* field of a trs structure contains a *memory pointer*. A memory pointer is a union (variant record) type possessing pointers of each of the three basic data types for the APL system: real, integer, and character. These three fields are denoted rp, ip, and cp, respectively. Since it is known that the result will be an integer, the ip field can be used directly in both the trs value trs1 and memory pointer value *mp1*.

Since it can be determined at compile time that the result is a scalar, no loop is generated. Instead, the single integer value is produced and copied into the memory pointed to by the memory pointer value *mp1*. This integer value is produced in the variable named *res15.i*.

The last act of the code for assignment is to free the storage used by the previous value assigned to the variable A (if there was a previous value) and to bind the new values to the name. This is accomplished by calling the procedure *assign*.

First Reduction

The outermost reduction function generates the following code:

Shape Phase

```
i20 = 200;
```

Value Phase

```
res15.i = 0;
for (i3 = 0; i3 < i20; i3++) {
 . . .
     res15.i += . . .
}
```

During the shape phase the size of the vector being reduced (200) is computed and placed into the counter *i20*. During the value phase the offset to be passed to the subexpression is computed in a loop running from 0 to this value. The expression *i3*++ is a C idiom for incrementing the value of *i3* by 1.

The variable *res15* is used to maintain the running sum of the reduction. As with memory pointers, result variables can contain any of the three basic datatypes: real, integer, or character. The i field indicates that an integer value is being used in the present case. The result variable is initialized prior to the loop to the value 0, which is the identity for the addition operator. The variable is then incremented once during each iteration of the loop. The operator += is once more a C idiom, resulting in the left argument being incremented by the value on the right side.

Note that this code takes advantage of the fact that addition is commutative. If a noncommutative function, such as subtraction, had been used instead, it would have necessitated making two changes to the generated code. The first would be that the loop would have to run backwards, instead of forwards. Secondly, instead of using the efficient C increment instruction, the code would look something like this:

```
res15.i = . . . - res15.i;
```

The Constant 2 and the Equality Function

The constant 2 and the outermost equality function together generate almost no code, being combined with the result of the inner reduction and the updating of the outer reduction. Note that == is the C operator for equality test and produces either a 0 or 1 value. Lazy code generation results in the code for the constant 2, the test for equality, and the updating of the running sum for the reduction operator all being performed in a single C statement.

```
res15.i += (2 == res11.i);
```

The Second Reduction Function

We have already noted that the index for the value being requested of the reduction is contained in the counter *i3*, and the result is placed in the variable *res11*. The rest of the code for the reduction is as follows:

Shape Phase

```
i13 = 200;
i12 = 200;
i15 = (i13 - 1) * i12;
```

Value Phase

```
res11.i = 0;
i4 = i15 + i3;
for (i14 = i13 - 1; i14 >= 0; i14--) {
    ...
    res11.i += ...
    i4 -= i12;
}
```

The variables *i13* and *i12* are initialized during the shape phase to the length of the row being reduced and the expansion vector value for the axis being reduced, respectively. (In terms of the quantities described in Chapter 5, these are the values s_i and e_i) The variable *i15* is the loop invariant expression $(s_i - 1)e_i$, which would otherwise be recomputed each time a new value was requested from the reduction.

The variable *i4* is the index of the position being requested from the subexpression. It should not be confused with variable *i14*, which is merely a counter insuring that the loop is executed the required number of times. The computation to initialize *i4* corresponds to

$$offset' = ((s_i - 1)e_i) + offset$$

After each iteration of the loop the index *i4* is updated to point to the next value. Note the differences between the code generated for this reduction and that generated for the previous reduction. There are two reasons for these differences: one is the fact that the outer reduction is accessed in sequential fashion and this one is not, and the second is that the outer reduction is iterating over a vector, whereas this reduction is operating on an object of higher dimension.

The Inner Scalar Equality Function

Like the first scalar equality test, the constant 0 and the scalar equality test are combined with code generated by other functions.

```
.. (0 == · · · )
```

The Outer Product

During the shape phase, the size of the right side of the outer product is computed and placed in the variable *i9*. This value is then used to convert the offset for the requested element, *i4*, into offsets for the left and right sides (*i5* and *i6*, respectively). Note that combining the computation of the divisor and remainder together results in a small increase in efficiency, since the generated assembly language can avoid having to reload the variable *i5*.

Shape Phase

```
i9 =200
```

Value Phase

```
i6 =i4 – i9 * (i5 =i4 / i9);
 · · · % · · ·
```

In this particular case, the APL function residue corresponds to the C operator mod (%) with the arguments reversed. Since the types of the arguments are known, the code can be combined with other expressions.

The Iotas

The code generated for the iota functions merely take the index of the desired element and add 1 (the index origin) to them. If the index origin is not known at compile time, code is generated to add the value of the global variable maintaining the index origin, *_ixorg*, into the expression. Once more, lazy code generation permits us to combine the code for both the iotas, the outer product, the equality test against the constant zero, and the updating of the value for the running sum of the inner reduction.

```
res11.i +=(0 ==((i6 +1) % (i5 +1)));
```

With Less Information

Suppose instead of the constant 200, the upper limit for the iota functions had been given by an identifier, as in

```
A ← +/ (2 =+⌿0 =(ι N) ∘.| ι N)
```

It is instructive to note that in this case all the code between the call on *settrs* and the call on *assign* would remain unchanged, and only the code generated for the shape phase would be altered. As this code contributes to only a small fraction of the execution time, the result would be only marginally slower.

Here is the new code that would be generated for the shape phase in this case:

```
if (n.type ==UKTYPE) error("undefined value used");
mp4 =n.value;
if (n.type !=INT) error("type error");
if (n.rank !=0) error("rank error");
mp2 =n.value;
outershape(&mp6, 1, mp4.ip, 1, mp2.ip);
i9 =*mp2.ip;
i13 =*mp6.ip;
i12 =esubi(0, 2, mp6.ip);
i15 =(i13 - 1) * i12;
i20 =*(mp6.ip +1);
settrs(&trs1, INT, 0, &i_main[1]);
```

The variables *mp4* and *mp2* hold the size of the vector produced by the iota function. Observe that no attempt is made by the APL compiler to determine common subexpressions, thus the fact that *mp4* and *mp2* contain the same information, and thus the variables *i9* and *i13* as well, is not noted nor made use of. (Common subexpressions tend to be rather rare in both APL code and the code generated by the compiler.) The function *outershape* computes the shape of the outer product. The function *esubi* computes the value e_1.

If N is declared to be scalar, the test for the rank disappears. If N is declared to be integer, the test for type disappears. If N is declared to be both scalar and integer, the code is simplified to the following:

```
if (n.type == UKTYPE) error("undefined value used");
outershape(&mp6, 1, n.value.ip, 1, n.value.ip);
i9 = *n.value.ip;
i13 = *mp6.ip;
i12 = esubi(0, 2, mp6.ip);
i15 = (i13 - 1) * i12;
i20 = *(mp6.ip + 1);
settrs(&trs1, INT, 0, &i_main[1]);
```

Compression

If we now go back and consider the original primes idiom, which returned the prime values instead of merely computing their number, we can see how the shape phase of one operation may include the value phase of others. This expression can be written as follows:

A ← (2 = +⌿0 = (ι 200) ∘.| ι 200) / ι 200

Notice that the only difference between this expression and the earlier one is the use of compression over an iota rather than a reduction.

The code generated for this statement is as follows:

```
i22 =0;
i9 =200;
i13 =200;
i12 =200;
i15 =(i13 - 1) * i12;
i19 =0;
i21 =200;
valloc(&mp11, i21, INT);
for (i3 =0; i3 < i21; i3++) {
      res11.i =0;
      i4 =i15 +i3;
      for (i14 =i13 - 1; i14 >=0; i14--) {
            i6 =i4 - i9 * (i5 =i4 / i9);
            res11.i +=(0 ==((i6 +1) % (i5 +1)));
            i4 -=i12;
      }
      if (((2 ==res11.i) !=0))
            *(mp11.ip +i22++) =i3;
}
valloc(&mp12, 1, INT);
*mp12.ip =i22;
settrs(&trs1, INT, 1, mp12.ip);
i1 =talloc(&trs1);
mp1.ip =trs1.value.ip;
for (i2 =0; i2 < i1; i2++) {
      i23 =*(mp11.ip +i2);
      (*mp1.ip++ =(i23 +1));
}
assign(&A, &trs1);
memfree(&mp12.ip);
memfree(&mp11.ip);
```

Notice how the change from a reduction to a compression has significantly changed the structure of the generated code. There are now two different distinct loops: one produced by the compression function during its shape phase and one produced by the assignment function. The majority of the computation now takes place during the shape phase code for the compression function. This code is as follows:

Shape Phase

```
i22 =0;
 . . .
valloc(&mp11, i21, INT);
for (i3 =0; i3 < i21; i3++) {
 . . .
        if (((2 ==res11.i) !=0))
              *(mp11.ip +i22++) =i3;
}
valloc(&mp12, 1, INT);
*mp12.ip =i22;
```

The variable *i22* is a counter. When the shape phase loop generated by the compression is finished, it will contain the number of nonzero values encountered and thus the length along the compressed axis of the resulting expression. In order to create space to hold the vector that will represent the positions of the nozeron values along the compressed axis, the memory pointer *mp11* is passed to the memory allocation routine *valloc*. The compress function then creates a loop to gather the values of the left argument. As each value is produced, it is compared against 0 (!= is the C not-equal comparison operator). If it is not 0, *i22* is incremented and the position of the nonzero element is stored in the vector pointed to by *mp11*.

When the loop generated by the compress function is finished, the value *i22* contains the length of the compressed axis in the result expression, and *mp11* points to a vector indicating the positions in the original ordering (the right argument) that correspond to the nonzero positions. A shape vector for the result is created by calling *valloc* once more, and the shape of the result is placed into it. (Since the result is a scalar, this is a simple assignment.) The assignment function then generates a loop to gather the results of the compression: Inside this loop, the compression function generates an index into the vector previously stored in *mp11*, which yields the position in the right argument where the result will be found. Since the result is given by an iota function, it can be easily computed by adding 1 (the index origin) to the requested position.

Value Phase

```
i23 =*(mp11.ip +i2);
(*mp1.ip++ =(i23 +1));
```

Finally, following the rebinding of the variable value generated by the assignment function, the compression function releases the memory used by the two vectors, the position vector and the shape vector.

A Critique

These examples illustrate one of the drawbacks of the APL compiler. Namely, no matter how many optimization techniques are applied to the generated code, they cannot make any change to the underlying algorithm. (One cannot change a Bubble sort into a Quick sort by any sequence of mechanical transformations.) The language APL strongly influences a programmer towards a style of programming that is often not as efficient as possible. For example, while one can usually write $O(n)$ or $O(n^2)$ algorithms easily in APL, it is difficult to write $O(n \log n)$ algorithms. A programmer setting about to solve a similar problem in C would probably not use this idiom at all, as natural as it is in APL, but would instead likely employ some variation on a sieve algorithm. While still an $O(n^2)$ solution, in practice it can be made much more efficient.

This observation should not be construed as being damning to APL or indeed to the APL compiler, any more than the observation that assembly language programmers can usually write more efficient programs than programmers in high level languages implies that nobody should write in high level languages. In both cases, the advantage of the higher level language is that it simplifies and facilitates the construction of bug free, correct code. Oftentimes, this is the primary concern, with efficiency only a distant second issue.

Appendix 3

A Longer Example

In this appendix we present, without commentary, the complete C program produced for the Ulam Spiral of Primes functions described in Chapter 2.

```
#include "aplc.h"
extern struct trs_struct n;
int i_spiral[15] ={
   0, 1, 2, 4, 2, -1, 4, 0, 2, 1,
   1, 2, 3, 2, 0}
;
double r_spiral[1] ={
   0.5}
;
spiral(z, _no2, l)
struct trs_struct *z, *_no2, *l;
{
   struct trs_struct e;
   struct trs_struct g;
   struct trs_struct c;
```

```
struct trs_struct a;
struct trs_struct trs1, trs2, trs3, trs4;
union mp_struct mp1, mp2, mp3, mp4, mp5, mp6, mp7, mp8, mp9,
mp10, mp11, mp12, mp13, mp14, mp15, mp16, mp17, mp18, mp19,
mp20, mp21, mp22, mp23, mp24, mp25, mp26, mp27, mp28, mp29,
mp30, mp31, mp32;
union res_struct res1, res2, res3, res4, res5, res6, res7, res8, res9,
res10, res11, res12, res13, res14, res15, res16, res17, res18, res19,
res20, res21, res22;
int i0, i1, i2, i3, i4, i5, i6, i7, i8, i9,
i10, i11, i12, i13, i14, i15, i16, i17, i18, i19,
i20, i21, i22, i23, i24, i25, i26, i27, i28, i29,
i30, i31, i32, i33, i34, i35, i36, i37, i38, i39,
i40, i41, i42, i43;

e.type = UKTYPE;
g.type = UKTYPE;
c.type = UKTYPE;
a.type = UKTYPE;

stmtno = 1;
while (stmtno)
   switch(stmtno) {
   default:
      stmtno = 0;
      break;
   case 1:
      stmtno = 1;
      trace("spiral", 1);
      if (n.type == UKTYPE) error("undefined value used");
      valloc(&mp5, 1, INT);
      *mp5.ip = (*n.value.ip * 2);
      i6 = _ixorg;
      settrs(&trs1, INT, 1, mp5.ip);
      i1 = talloc(&trs1);
      mp1.ip = trs1.value.ip;
      for (i2 = 0; i2 < i1; i2++) {
         (*mp1.ip++ = i6++);
      }
      assign(&a, &trs1);
      memfree(&mp5.ip);
   case 2:
      stmtno = 2;
      trace("spiral", 2);
      if (a.type == UKTYPE) error("undefined value used");
      mp2.ip = a.value.ip;
      settrs(&trs2, INT, 1, a.shape);
```

```
    trs2.value.ip = mp2.ip;
    i7 = 1;
    i8 = *a.shape;
    i10 = *a.shape;
    valloc(&mp6, i10, INT);
    mp7 = mp6;
    for (i5 = 0; i5 < i10; i5++) {
        res5.i = 0;
        for (i9 = i5; i9 >= 0; i9--) {
            (res5.i = (*(a.value.ip + i9) - res5.i));
        }
        if (res5.i < 0)
            res5.i = - res5.i;
        (*mp6.ip++ = res5.i);
    }
    settrs(&trs3, INT, 1, a.shape);
    trs3.value.ip = mp7.ip;
    copies(&trs4, &trs2, &trs3);
    mp8.ip = trs4.value.ip;
    settrs(&trs1, INT, 1, trs4.shape);
    i1 = talloc(&trs1);
    mp1.ip = trs1.value.ip;
    for (i2 = 0; i2 < i1; i2++) {
        (*mp1.ip++ = (*mp8.ip++ % 4));
    }
    assign(&c, &trs1);
    memfree(&mp7.ip);
case 3:
    stmtno = 3;
    trace("spiral", 3);
    if (n.type == UKTYPE) error("undefined value used");
    settrs(&trs1, INT, 0, &i_spiral[1]);
    i1 = talloc(&trs1);
    mp1.ip = trs1.value.ip;
    {
        (*mp1.ip = ((int) floor((r_spiral[0] +
            (((double) *n.value.ip) / ((double) 2))))));
    }
    assign(&g, &trs1);
case 4:
    stmtno = 4;
    trace("spiral", 4);
    if (l->type == UKTYPE) error("undefined value used");
    valloc(&mp3, 1, INT);
    *mp3.ip = *l->shape;
    if (n.type == UKTYPE) error("undefined value used");
    i17 = 1;
```

```
    valloc(&mp15, i17, INT);
    mp16 = mp15;
    {
        (*mp15.ip = ((*n.value.ip * *n.value.ip) - 1));
    }
    if (c.type == UKTYPE) error("undefined value used");
    i8 = 1;
    valloc(&mp9, i8, INT);
    for (i9 = i8 - 1; i9 >= 0; i9--) {
        *(mp9.ip + i9) = iabs(*(mp16.ip + i9));
    }
    i10 = qsdalloc(1, &mp5, &mp6, &mp7);
    i9 = 0;
    {
        if (*(mp16.ip + i9) < 0)
            *(mp6.ip + i9) += *(c.shape + i9) + *(mp16.ip + i9);
    }
    i7 = accessor(1, mp9.ip, 1, c.shape, &mp8, mp5.ip, mp6.ip, mp7.ip);
    outershape(&mp24, 1, mp3.ip, 1, mp9.ip);
    i24 = *mp9.ip;
    settrs(&trs1, INT, 2, mp24.ip);
    i1 = talloc(&trs1);
    mp1.ip = trs1.value.ip;
    for (i2 = 0; i2 < i1; i2++) {
        i6 = i2 % i24;
        i8 = i6;
        i11 = i7;
        for (i9 = i10 - 1; i9 >= 0; i9--) {
            i11 += i8 * *(mp8.ip + i9);
            i8 /= *(mp9.ip + i9);
        }
        i4 = i2 / i24;

        i3 = (((*(c.value.ip + i11) + ((0 == *(c.value.ip + i11)) * 4))
            + (i4 * *(l->shape + 1))) - _ixorg);
        (*mp1.ip++ = *(l->value.ip + i3));
    }
    assign(&e, &trs1);
    memfree(&mp3.ip);
    memfree(&mp4.ip);
    memfree(&mp24.ip);
case 5:
    stmtno = 5;
    trace("spiral", 5);
    if (n.type == UKTYPE) error("undefined value used");
    i8 = 2;
    valloc(&mp6, i8, INT);
```

```
mp7 = mp6;
for (i3 = 0; i3 < i8; i3++) {
   (*mp6.ip++ = *n.value.ip);
}
trs2.type = UKTYPE;
mp13.ip = &i_spiral[9];
if (g.type == UKTYPE) error("undefined value used");
if (e.type == UKTYPE) error("undefined value used");
mp18.ip = e.value.ip;
catshape(&mp16, 0, &i_spiral[1], 2, e.shape);
i25 = 1;
i28 = *(e.shape + 1);
i27 = i25 + i28;
i34 = *(mp16.ip + 1);
i35 = i34;
i36 = vsize(2, mp16.ip);
valloc(&mp19, i36, INT);
mp20 = mp19;
for (i22 = 0; i22 < i36; i22++) {
   if (i35 >= i34) {
      res12.i = 0;
      i35 = 0;
   }
   i29 = i22 % i27;
   if (i29 < i25) {
      (res9.i = 0);
   }
   else {
      (res9.i = *mp18.ip++ );
   }
   res12.i += res9.i;
   i35++;
   (*mp19.ip++ = res12.i);
}
outershape(&mp25, 1, &i_spiral[13], 2, mp16.ip);
i41 = vsize(2, mp16.ip);
dtshape(&mp12, &i_spiral[9], 3, mp25.ip);
i16 = qsdalloc(2, &mp8, &mp9, &mp10);
dtmerge(&i_spiral[9], 3, &mp8, &mp9, &mp10);
i13 = accessor(2, mp12.ip, 3, mp25.ip, &mp11, mp8.ip,
   mp9.ip, mp10.ip);
i17 = i13;
i42 = vsize(2, mp12.ip);
valloc(&mp26, i42, INT);
mp27 = mp26;
for (i12 = 0; i12 < i42; i12++) {
   i21 = i17 - i41 * (i20 = i17 / i41);
```

```
                getmp(&res13, &mp20, i21, INT);
                cktype(&res13, INT, INT);
                (res6.i =(*g.value.ip +res13.i));
                i14 =*((i16 +mp12.ip) - 1);
                for (i15 =i16 - 1; i15 >=0; i15--) {
                    i17 +=*(mp11.ip +i15);
                    if (0 ==((i12 +1) % i14))
                        i14 *=*((i15 +mp12.ip) - 1);
                    else
                        break;
                }
                (*mp26.ip++ =res6.i);
            }
            settrs(&trs3, INT, 2, mp12.ip);
            trs3.value.ip =mp27.ip;
            linear(&trs4, &trs2, &trs3);
            mp28 =trs4.value;
            if (trs4.rank !=1) error("rank error");
            aplsort(&mp31, &mp28, *trs4.shape, trs4.type, 1);
            i10 =*trs4.shape;
            settrs(&trs1, INT, 2, mp7.ip);
            i1 =talloc(&trs1);
            mp1.ip =trs1.value.ip;
            for (i2 =0; i2 < i1; i2++) {
                i9 =i2 % i10;
                (*mp1.ip++ =(*(mp31.ip +i9) +_ixorg));
            }
            assign(z, &trs1);
            memfree(&mp7.ip);
            memfree(&mp27.ip);
            memfree(&mp20.ip);
            memfree(&mp16.ip);
            memfree(&mp25.ip);
            memfree(&mp31.ip);
            stmtno =0;
        }
}
int i_copies[5] ={
    0, 1, -1, 1, 0}
;
copies(c, a, b)
struct trs_struct *c, *a, *b;
{
    struct trs_struct trs1;
    union mp_struct mp1, mp2, mp3, mp4, mp5, mp6, mp7, mp8, mp9,
    mp10, mp11, mp12, mp13, mp14, mp15, mp16, mp17, mp18, mp19,
    mp20, mp21, mp22, mp23, mp24, mp25;
```

```
union res_struct res1, res2, res3, res4, res5, res6, res7, res8, res9,
res10, res11, res12, res13, res14, res15, res16, res17, res18, res19,
res20;
int i0, i1, i2, i3, i4, i5, i6, i7, i8, i9,
i10, i11, i12, i13, i14, i15, i16, i17, i18, i19,
i20, i21, i22, i23, i24, i25, i26, i27, i28, i29,
i30, i31, i32, i33, i34, i35, i36, i37, i38, i39;


stmtno = 1;
while (stmtno)
  switch(stmtno) {
  default:
    stmtno = 0;
    break;
  case 1:
    stmtno = 1;
    trace("copies", 1);
    if (a->type == UKTYPE) error("undefined value used");
    if (b->type == UKTYPE) error("undefined value used");
    mp3.ip = b->value.ip;
    i7 = *b->shape;
    res4.i = 0;
    for (i5 = 0; i5 < i7; i5++) {
      res4.i += *mp3.ip++;
    }
    valloc(&mp5, 1, INT);
    *mp5.ip = res4.i;
    i11 = _ixorg;
    catshape(&mp14, 0, &i_copies[1], 1, b->shape);
    i22 = 1;
    i25 = *b->shape;
    i24 = i22 + i25;
    i29 = 1;
    i30 = *mp14.ip;
    i14 = 1;
    valloc(&mp10, i14, INT);
    for (i15 = i14 - 1; i15 >= 0; i15--) {
      *(mp10.ip + i15) = *(mp14.ip + i15) - iabs(i_copies[(i15 + 2)]);
    }
    i16 = qsdalloc(1, &mp6, &mp7, &mp8);
    i13 = accessor(1, mp10.ip, 1, mp14.ip, &mp9, mp6.ip,
      mp7.ip, mp8.ip);
    i17 = i13;
    valloc(&mp19, 1, INT);
    i34 = *mp10.ip;
```

```
*mp19.ip =i34;
i35 =*mp19.ip;
valloc(&mp20, i35, INT);
mp21 =mp20;
for (i12 =0; i12 < i35; i12++) {
   res12.i =0;
   for (i31 =i17; i31 >=0; i31--) {
      i26 =i31;
      if (i26 < i22) {
         (res9.i =0);
      }
      else {
         i26 -=i22;
         (res9.i =*(b->value.ip +i26));
      }
      res12.i +=res9.i;
   }
   (res6.i =(res12.i +1));
   i14 =*((i16 +mp10.ip) - 1);
   for (i15 =i16 - 1; i15 >=0; i15--) {
      i17 +=*(mp9.ip +i15);
      if (0 ==((i12 +1) % i14))
         i14 *=*((i15 +mp10.ip) - 1);
      else
         break;
   }
   (*mp20.ip++ =res6.i);
}
aplsort(&mp22, &mp21, *mp19.ip, INT, 1);
i37 =*mp5.ip;
res19.i =0;
settrs(&trs1, INT, 1, mp5.ip);
i1 =talloc(&trs1);
mp1.ip =trs1.value.ip;
for (i2 =0; i2 < i1; i2++) {
   (res18.i =i11++);
   res18.i =aplsearch(mp22.ip, &mp21, &res18,
      INT, *mp19.ip) < *mp19.ip;
   res19.i +=res18.i;
   i3 =(res19.i - _ixorg);
   (*mp1.ip++ =*(a->value.ip +i3));
}
assign( c, &trs1);
memfree(&mp5.ip);
memfree(&mp21.ip);
memfree(&mp14.ip);
memfree(&mp19.ip);
```

```
        memfree(&mp22.ip);
        memfree(&mp25.ip);
        stmtno = 0;
    }
}
int i_primes[5] = {
  0, 1, 2, 0, 2}
;
primes(x, _no2, a)
struct trs_struct *x, *_no2, *a;
{
  struct trs_struct s;
  struct trs_struct trs1;
  union mp_struct mp1, mp2, mp3, mp4, mp5, mp6, mp7, mp8, mp9,
  mp10, mp11, mp12, mp13, mp14, mp15, mp16, mp17, mp18, mp19,
  mp20, mp21, mp22;
  union res_struct res1, res2, res3, res4, res5, res6, res7, res8, res9,
  res10, res11, res12, res13, res14, res15, res16, res17, res18, res19,
  res20, res21, res22;
  int i0, i1, i2, i3, i4, i5, i6, i7, i8, i9,
  i10, i11, i12, i13, i14, i15, i16, i17, i18, i19,
  i20, i21, i22, i23, i24, i25, i26, i27;

  s.type = UKTYPE;

  stmtno = 1;
  while (stmtno)
    switch(stmtno) {
    default:
      stmtno = 0;
      break;
    case 1:
      stmtno = 1;
      trace("primes", 1);
      if (a->type == UKTYPE) error("undefined value used");
      mp4.ip = a->shape;
      i5 = 2;
      settrs(&trs1, INT, 0, &i_primes[1]);
      i1 = talloc(&trs1);
      mp1.ip = trs1.value.ip;
      {
        res3.i = 1;
        for (i3 = 0; i3 < i5; i3++) {
          res3.i *= *mp4.ip++;
        }
        (*mp1.ip = res3.i);
      }
```

```
      assign(&s, &trs1);
   case 2:
      stmtno =2;
      trace("primes", 2);
      mp2.ip =a->value.ip;
      i23 =0;
      if (s.type ==UKTYPE) error("undefined value used");
      outershape(&mp7, 1, s.value.ip, 1, s.value.ip);
      i10 =*s.value.ip;
      i14 =*mp7.ip;
      i13 =*(mp7.ip +1);
      i16 =(i14 - 1) * i13;
      i20 =0;
      i22 =*(s.value.ip +i20);
      valloc(&mp13, i22, INT);
      for (i4 =0; i4 < i22; i4++) {
         res12.i =0;
         i5 =i16 +i4;
         for (i15 =i14 - 1; i15 >=0; i15--) {
            i7 =i5 - i10 * (i6 =i5 / i10);
            res12.i +=(0 ==((i7 +_ixorg) % (i6 +_ixorg)));
            i5 -=i13;
         }
         if (((2 ==res12.i) !=0))
            *(mp13.ip +i23++) =i4;
      }
      memfree(&mp7.ip);
      valloc(&mp14, 1, INT);
      *mp14.ip =i23;
      valloc(&mp17, 1, INT);
      i26 =*mp14.ip;
      *mp17.ip =i26;
      i27 =*mp17.ip;
      valloc(&mp18, i27, INT);
      mp19 =mp18;
      for (i3 =0; i3 < i27; i3++) {
         i24 =*(mp13.ip +i3);
         (*mp18.ip++ =(i24 +_ixorg));
      }
      aplsort(&mp20, &mp19, *mp17.ip, INT, 1);
      settrs(&trs1, BIT, 2, a->shape);
      i1 =talloc(&trs1);
      mp1.ip =trs1.value.ip;
      for (i2 =0; i2 < i1; i2++) {
         (res22.i =*mp2.ip++ );
         res22.i =aplsearch(mp20.ip, &mp19, &res22,
            INT, *mp17.ip) < *mp17.ip;
```

```
            (*mp1.ip++ =res22.i);
        }
        assign( x, &trs1);
        memfree(&mp19.ip);
        memfree(&mp14.ip);
        memfree(&mp13.ip);
        memfree(&mp17.ip);
        memfree(&mp20.ip);
        stmtno =0;
    }
}
int i_linear[4] ={
  0, 1, 1, 1}
;
linear(l, _no2, m)
struct trs_struct *l, *_no2, *m;
{
  struct trs_struct trs1;
  union mp_struct mp1, mp2, mp3, mp4, mp5, mp6, mp7, mp8;
  union res_struct res1, res2, res3, res4, res5, res6, res7, res8, res9,
  res10, res11, res12, res13, res14;
  int i0, i1, i2, i3, i4, i5, i6, i7, i8, i9,
  i10, i11, i12;


  stmtno =1;
  while (stmtno)
    switch(stmtno) {
    default:
      stmtno =0;
      break;
    case 1:
      stmtno =1;
      trace("linear", 1);
      if (n.type ==UKTYPE) error("undefined value used");
      if (m->type ==UKTYPE) error("undefined value used");
      innershape(&mp2, 0, &i_linear[1], 2, m->shape);
      i8 =*m->shape;
      i9 =*(m->shape +1);
      i8--;
      i10 =i8 * i9;
      settrs(&trs1, INT, 1, mp2.ip);
      i1 =talloc(&trs1);
      mp1.ip =trs1.value.ip;
      for (i2 =0; i2 < i1; i2++) {
        i5 =i2 - i9 * (i4 =i2 / i9);
        i5 +=i10;
```

```
            res11.i = 0;
            res2.i = 1;
            for (i3 = i8; i3 >= 0; i3--) {
                (res3.i = (res2.i * (*(m->value.ip + i5) - 1)));
                res2.i *= *n.value.ip;
                res11.i += res3.i;
                i5 -= i9;
            }
            (*mp1.ip++ = (res11.i + 1));
        }
        assign( l, &trs1);
        stmtno = 0;
    }
}
int i_timeit[18] = {
    0, 1, 0, 2, 1, 2, 4, 2, -1, 0,
    1, 0, 0, 1, 0, -1, 8, 1}
;
char c_timeit[] = " *";
int l_timeit[1] = {
    2}
;
timeit(_no1, _no2, w)
struct trs_struct *_no1, *_no2, *w;
{
    struct trs_struct x;
    struct trs_struct i;
    struct trs_struct trs1, trs2, trs3, trs4, trs5, trs6, trs7;
    union mp_struct mp1, mp2, mp3, mp4, mp5, mp6, mp7, mp8, mp9,
    mp10, mp11, mp12, mp13, mp14, mp15;
    union res_struct res1, res2, res3, res4, res5, res6, res7, res8, res9,
    res10, res11, res12, res13;
    int i0, i1, i2, i3, i4, i5, i6, i7, i8, i9,
    i10, i11, i12;

    x.type = UKTYPE;
    i.type = UKTYPE;

    stmtno = 1;
    while (stmtno)
        switch(stmtno) {
        default:
            stmtno = 0;
            break;
        case 1:
            stmtno = 1;
            trace("timeit", 1);
```

```
        settrs(&trs1, BIT, 0, &i_timeit[1]);
        i1 = talloc(&trs1);
        mp1.ip = trs1.value.ip;
        {
           (*mp1.ip = 0);
        }
        assign(&i, &trs1);
    case 2:
        stmtno = 2;
        trace("timeit", 2);
        trs5.type = UKTYPE;
        trs2.type = UKTYPE;
        mp6.ip = &i_timeit[8];
        settrs(&trs3, INT, 2, &i_timeit[5]);
        trs3.value.ip = &i_timeit[8];
        spiral(&trs4, &trs2, &trs3);
        mp9.ip = trs4.value.ip;
        settrs(&trs6, INT, 2, trs4.shape);
        trs6.value.ip = mp9.ip;
        primes(&trs7, &trs5, &trs6);
        mp12.ip = trs7.value.ip;
        settrs(&trs1, CHAR, 2, trs7.shape);
        i1 = talloc(&trs1);
        mp1.cp = trs1.value.cp;
        for (i2 = 0; i2 < i1; i2++) {
           i3 = ((*mp12.ip++ + 1) - _ixorg);
           (*mp1.cp++ = c_timeit[i3]);
        }
        assign(&x, &trs1);
        memfree(&mp15.ip);
    case 3:
        stmtno = 3;
        trace("timeit", 3);
        if (i.type == UKTYPE) error("undefined value used");
        settrs(&trs1, INT, 0, &i_timeit[1]);
        i1 = talloc(&trs1);
        mp1.ip = trs1.value.ip;
        {
           (*mp1.ip = (*i.value.ip + 1));
        }
        assign(&i, &trs1);
    case 4:
        stmtno = 4;
        trace("timeit", 4);
        if (w->type == UKTYPE) error("undefined value used");
        mp1 = w->value;
        if (w->rank != 0) error("rank error");
```

```
        i2 =0;
        getmp(&res1, &mp1, ((w->rank) ? i2 : 0), w->type);
        (res3.i =*i.value.ip);
        dsopv(LT, &res3, &res3, INT, &res1, w->type);
        valloc(&mp4, 1, INT);
        *mp4.ip =res3.i;
        i5 =_ixorg;
        i8 =*mp4.ip;
        if (i8 > 0) {
           i1 =0;
           stmtno =(l_timeit[0] * i5++);
           break;
        }
        memfree(&mp4.ip);
        stmtno =0;
    }
}
struct trs_struct n;
int i_main[4] ={
   0, 1, 10, 10}
;
main() {
   struct trs_struct trs1, trs2, trs3;
   union mp_struct mp1, mp2, mp3, mp4;
   union res_struct res1, res2, res3;
   int i0, i1, i2;

   n.type =UKTYPE;

   stmtno =1;
   while (stmtno)
      switch(stmtno) {
      default:
         stmtno =0;
         break;
      case 1:
         stmtno =1;
         trace("main", 1);
         settrs(&trs1, INT, 0, &i_main[1]);
         i1 =talloc(&trs1);
         mp1.ip =trs1.value.ip;
         {
            (*mp1.ip =10);
         }
         assign(&n, &trs1);
      case 2:
         stmtno =2;
```

```
        trace("main", 2);
        trs1.type =UKTYPE;
        settrs(&trs2, INT, 0, &i_main[1]);
        trs2.value.ip =&i_main[3];
        timeit(&trs3, &trs1, &trs2);
        stmtno =0;
    }
}
```

References

Abelson, Harold, and Sussman, Gerald Jay, 1985. *Structure and Interpretation of Computer Programs.* MIT Press, Cambridge, Massachusetts

Aho, Alfred V., Sethi, Ravi, and Ullman, Jeffery D., 1986. *Compilers: Principles, Techniques, and Tools.* Addison-Wesley, Reading, Massachusetts.

Budd, Timothy A., 1987. *A Little Smalltalk.* Addison-Wesley, Reading, Massachusetts.

Dijkstra, Edsger W.: 1972. "The Humble Programmer," in *Communications of the ACM,* Vol 15(10): 859-866 (This is the 1972 ACM Turing Award Lecture.)

Gabriel, Richard P.: 1986. *Performance and Evaluation of Lisp Systems,* MIT Press, Cambridge, Massachusetts

Gilman, L., and Rose, A., 1976. *APL an Interactive Approach*, Wiley, New York.

Guibas, Leo J., and Wyatt, Douglas K., 1978. Compilation and Delayed Evaluation in APL. *Conference Record of the Fifth Annual ACM Symposium on Principles of Programming Languages*, Tucson, Arizona.

Hanson, David R., 1983. Simple Code Optimizations. *Software-Practice and Experience*, Vol 13: 745-763.

Iverson, Kenneth E., 1980. Notation as a Tool of Thought. *Communications of the ACM*, Vol 23(8): 444-465. (This is the 1979 ACM Turing Award Lecture.)

Knuth, Donald E., 1971. An Empirical Study of FORTRAN Programs. *Software-Practice and Experience*, Vol 1: 105-133.

Miller, Terrence C., 1979. Type Checking in an Imperfect World. *Conference Record of the Sixth Annual ACM Symposium on Principles of Programming Languages*, San Antonio, Texas.

Muchnick, Steven S., and Jones, Neil D. (eds), 1981. *Program Flow Analysis, Theory and Applications.* Prentice Hall, Englewood Cliffs, New Jersey.

Polivka, Raymond P., and Pakin, Sandra, 1975. *APL: The Language and Its Usage.* Prentice-Hall, Englewood Cliffs, New Jersey.

Perlis, Alan J., and Rugaber, S., 1979. Programming with Idioms in APL. *APL Quote Quad*, Vol 9(4): 232-235.

Slade, Stephen, 1987. *The T Programming Language.* Prentice-Hall, Englewood Cliffs, New Jersey.

Waite, William M., and Goos, Gerhard, 1984. *Compiler Construction.* Springer-Verlag, New York.

Wiedmann, C., 1978. Steps Toward an APL Compiler. *APL Quote Quad*, Vol 9(4): 321-328.

Wilensky, Robert, 1984. *LISPcraft.* W. W. Norton, New York.

The following were not cited in the text, nevertheless, the reader may be interested in consulting them.

APL Compilation

Abrams, Philip S., 1970. *An APL Machine.* PhD Thesis, Stanford. SLAC Report No. 114.

Bauer, Alan M. and Saal, Harry J., 1974. Does APL Really Need Run-Time Checking? *Software—Practice and Experience,* Vol 4, 129-138.

Budd, Timothy A., 1984. The Design of an APL Compiler for a Vector Processor, *ACM Transactions on Programming Languages and Systems,* Vol 6(3): 297-312.

—, 1983. An APL Compiler for the UNIX Timesharing System. *APL Quote Quad,* Vol 13(3): 205-210.

—, 1985. Dataflow Analysis in APL. *APL Quote Quad,* Vol 15(4): 22-28.

—, and Treat, Joseph, 1984. Extensions to Grid Selector Composition and Compilation in APL, *Information Processing Letters,* Vol 19(3): 117-123.

Ching, Wai-Mee, 1981. A Design For Data Flow Analysis in an APL Compiler. Research Report RC 9151 (#40005.) IBM Thomas J. Watson Research Center, Yorktown Heights, New York.

—, 1986. An APL/370 Compiler and Some Performance Comparisons with APL Interpreter and FORTRAN. *APL Quote Quad,* Vol 16(4): 143-147.

Christopher, Thomas W. and Wallace, Ralph W., 1986. Compiling Optimized Array Expressions at Run-Time. *APL Quote-*

Quad, Vol. 16(4) 136-142.

Hassit, A. and Lyon, L.E., 1972. Efficient Evaluation of Array Subscripts of Arrays. *IBM Journal of Research and Development*, January 1972, 45-57.

Johnston, Ronald L., 1979. The Dynamic Incremental Compiler of APL\3000. *Proceedings of the APL 79 Conference*, Rochester, New York, 82-87

Miller, T. C., 1978. *Tentative Compilation: A Design for an APL Compiler*, PhD Thesis, Yale University, New Haven, Connecticut.

Naugle, Richard, 1986. APL Compilation and Interpretation by Translating to F83VEC. *APL Quote Quad*, Vol 16(4): 164-171.

Perlis, Alan J., 1974. Steps toward an APL Compiler. Computer Science Research Report 24, Yale University.

Roeder, Robert D., 1979. *Type Determination in an Optimizing Compiler for APL*, PhD Thesis, Iowa State University. (Available from University Microfilms International, Ann Arbor, Michigan.)

Saal, Harry J., 1978. Considerations in the Design of a Compiler for APL. *APL Quote-Quad*, Vol 8(4) 8-14. (includes an annotated bibliography).

—, and Weis, Z., 1975. Some Properties of APL Programs. *Proceedings of the APL 75 Conference.*

Strawn, G. O., 1977. Does APL Really Need Run-Time Parsing? *Software — Practice & Experience.* Vol 7: 193-200.

Sybalsky, J. D., 1980. An APL Compiler for the Production Environment. *APL80.* North-Holland Publishing Company.

Van Dyke, Eric J., 1977. A Dynamic Incremental Compiler for an Interpretive Language. Hewlett-Packard Journal, Vol 28(11)

17-23.

Weiss, Zvi, and Saal, Harry J., 1981. Compile Time Syntax Analysis of APL Programs. *APL Quote Quad*, Vol 12(1): 313-320.

Wiedmann, C., 1983. A Performance Comparison Between an APL Interpreter and Compiler. *APL Quote Quad*, Vol 13(3): 211-217.

Implementation Techniques for Other Nontraditional Languages

Brooks, Rodney A., Gabriel, Richard P., and Steel, Guy L., 1982. An Optimizing Compiler for Lexically Scoped LISP. *SigPlan Notices*, Vol 17(6): 261-275.

Budd, Timothy A., 1987. *A Little Smalltalk*, Addison Wesley, Reading, Massachusetts.

Campbell, J.A. (ed), 1984. *Implementations of Prolog*, Wiley, New York.

Ellis, John R., 1986. *Bulldog: A Compiler for VLIW Architectures.* MIT Press, Cambridge, Massachusetts

Griswold, Ralph E., and Griswold, Madge T., 1987. *The Implementation of the Icon Programming Language.* Princeton University Press, Princeton, New Jersey.

Tenenbaum, Aaron M., 1974. Type Determination for Very High Level Languages. Courant Computer Science Report 3, Courant Institute of Mathematical Sciences.

Index